Praise for
Kanban Maturity Model: Evolving Fit-for-Purpose Organizations

W9-BEJ-541

Don't let the "maturity model" moniker scare you. Anderson and his team have once again created a masterful work of clarity and usability for every tier in the organization. Borrowing loosely from the venerable CMMI and leveraging Bozheva's modeling expertise, the KMM's elegant architecture is all about the practitioner and their desire to move along a path toward operational Zen. Each practice in the KMM is a condition of truth on that path. Stopping short of prescribing how to bring about the conditions, the KMM offers plenty of tips and critical rationale to aid in internalizing the gestalt of Kanban and deeply absorbing its many benefits. I'm eager to see companies' implementations and the measurable impacts that result.

Hillel Glazer,
Author *High Performance Operations*

I found the Kanban Maturity Model extremely valuable to set the right expectations for my clients. It gives an organisation's management a perspective and high-level guidance on the way forward. As an experienced Kanban coach leading large-scale improvement initiatives, I value the model and its guidance for my day-to-day work on all levels. It is far more powerful than ticking of boxes. The KMM helps to look for evidence of value brought to the organisation. It is a must-read for every Kanban coach or agile practitioner.

Peter Kerschbaumer, Kanban Coaching Professional and
Enterprise Services Planning Trainer.

KMM is a map that helps us to locate where we are and define our path *toward better business results.*

Aitor Eguren, General Manager,
Soraluze Makina Bereziak, S.L.L.

KMM is a very useful and powerful complement to CMMI. In particular, its transition practices offer organizations an excellent way to define their improvement path, increase their maturity level, and overcome resistance to change. The model is very helpful for Lead Appraisers who evaluate organizations combining CMMI and Kanban. KMM should align nicely with CMMI 2.0. The addition of KMM maturity level 6 explicitly encourages organizations to take a serious look in the mirror, analyze their fitness to customer expectations, and revise their business model accordingly.

Giuseppe Satriani,
CMMI Lead Appraiser for High Maturity Level

The Kanban Maturity Model is a very valuable instrument for companies willing to continually improve the efficiency of their workflow and the quality of their services.

Gorka Galdona, Director of Maintenance Department,
Informatica68 S.A.

The Kanban Maturity Model helps you to understand where you are, shows what is possible and how to get there. It does so by explaining the observed behavior for each level and by what practices such behavior is encouraged. The Kanban Maturity Model has the potential to be the Rosetta Stone for organizational change with Kanban.

Wolfgang Wiedenroth, Accredited Kanban
Trainer and Coach, it-agile GmbH

If you're truly motivated to make long lasting evolutionary changes in your business and survive forthcoming disruptions in your industry, don't put this book down until you've reached the final page. Whether you're starting off with a general understanding of maturity with the Kanban Method or attempting to advance your organization's maturity to a higher level, this book will serve as a great guide and reference on your journey.

Joey Spooner, Kanban Coach and Trainer,
TriTech Enterprise Systems, Inc.

Clear, simple and precise model. An awesome book for all companies seeking organizational and business agility.

Juan J. Gil Bilbao,
Release Train Engineer, BBVA S.A.

Modern knowledge workers and managers operate in highly connected and networked organizations fraught with overburdened teams and high stress. The Kanban Maturity Model provides a lens through which to view these organizations as well as clear and actionable guidance on how to turn these new insights into positive change. This is the most practical and achievable path to organizational transformation and the achievement of business agility."

Jeremy Pullen,
Principal, Polodis Inc.

Kanban Maturity Model
Beta Release

Evolving Fit-for-Purpose Organizations

David J Anderson

Teodora Bozheva

LeanKanban
UNIVERSITY
P R E S S
Seattle, WA

Kanban Maturity Model: Evolving Fit For Purpose Organizations
Copyright © 2018 Lean Kanban University Press

ISBN: 978-0-9853051-5-4

First Print Edition, 7 April, 2018.

Contact info@leankanban.com for rights requests, customized editions, and bulk orders. Additional print copies of this and other Kanban publications can be purchased via leankanban.com/shop.

Library of Congress Cataloging-in-Publication Data
Applied for

Cover design by Armando Bayer Zabala
Interior design by Vicki Rowland

Printed in the United States

For Natalie —DJA

For Sergey, Bela, and George —TB

Contents

Part I | The Model

1 | Kanban Maturity Model Overview

Purpose

The purpose of the Kanban Maturity Model is to support the development of the following organizational capabilities:

- Relief from overburdening
- Delivering on customer expectations
- Organizational agility
- Predictable economic outcomes and financial robustness
- Survivability

The Kanban Maturity Model appears because reaching these outcomes is observed to be challenging for lots of organizations. It responds to the need for help to cope with resistance to change and to properly introduce the practices needed to make an entire organization resilient, robust, and ultimately antifragile.

With ten years of Kanban implementation experience around the world, it is now possible to codify why resistance happens and to provide prescriptive guidance on actions that can help build unity around common goals and improve work outcomes, including appropriateness of specific practices in the context of existing organizational maturity. The Model contains this codification and defines proven steps for correct practice implementation. In addition, it draws a roadmap to broader and deeper adoption over time. In particular, it clearly specifies the practices that can be introduced next with little resistance, or which, by design, produce just enough stress to cause the organization to react in an antifragile manner, resulting in improvement.

Influences and Integrations

The Kanban Maturity Model (KMM) is influenced by several management models that have preceded it. The KMM introduces a number of innovations, most notably a focus on business outcomes, and provides a number of mapping and integration points with existing models such as Capability Maturity Model Integration (CMMI™), Lean/TPS, Real World Risk Institute model, and Mission Command/*Auftragstaktik*. Its seven maturity levels are influenced by, and synthesize, concepts from Jerry Weinberg [6] and the CMMI[1][14].

Intended Users and Needs Addressed

Kanban coaches (Kanban Coaching Professionals, Kanban Coaching Masterclass alumni)

- Understand maturity level behaviors.

- Get useful guidelines for leading their customers' initiatives.

- Appraise the depth and breadth of a Kanban implementation.

- Determine appropriateness of certain practices.

- Define an approach for taking an organization to the next level; in particular, defining what to do next and how to stress the organization enough to provoke it to go to the next level.

- Explain to organizations what they can get from KMM, what happens when they are under stress, and from that, determine what would be the appropriate maturity level for the organization.

- Enhance professional credibility—avoid being seen as overly ambitious or lacking sufficient ambition.

Improvement initiative leaders and executives

- Develop a realistic roadmap for driving the initiative aligned to the organization's business objectives.

---

1. CMMI and Capability Maturity Model Integration are registered trademarks of the CMMI Institute.

- Clearly communicate the improvement initiative objectives, defined roadmap, concrete actions, and expected benefits to other managers and staff.

- Understand and measure the progress of the improvement initiative.

- Lead initiatives with confidence.

Agile practitioners and coaches

- Understand how Kanban practices can help to satisfy customers' expectations.

- Define a roadmap to develop further the organization's agility.

- Make customers see that there is more than one type of Kanban; understand the breadth and depth of Kanban and the values of using the method.

- All needs defined above.

Project and service managers

- Introduce appropriate practices that provide insight on and reveal information about the real state of their projects and services and enable better coordination of their teams' work.

- Learn how to improve project and service predictability.

- Apply effective practices that facilitate meeting customer expectations.

- Effectively manage shared resources.

- Effectively manage capacity so as to respond to changing service demand.

Benefits of the Kanban Maturity Model

- Helps managers and teams understand the system they manage and avoid making poor decisions that lead to negative effects on projects, services, people, customers, and business

- Describes a set of practices for use at enterprise scale; to avoid focusing on compliance to a framework, KMM does not define processes or a methodology—KMM's practices instead guide organizations toward fit-for-purpose products and services with appropriate exposure to risk and reasonable economic returns.

- Allows the objective assessment of the current state of an organization in order to see where challenges and opportunities lie on the path to greater business and organizational agility

- Provides guidelines on the improvement actions to take, creating just enough stress to catalyze improvement without overreaching and risking failure of adoption

- Helps benchmark organizational agility and fitness-for-purpose

- Improves positioning in the market by appropriately developing capabilities to satisfy and exceed customer expectations

- Aligns stakeholders and team members around a common understanding of the purpose of an improvement initiative and how to approach it

- Complements other models and methods, such as CMMI and PMBoK [14], with a systems thinking approach that incorporates an understanding of the psychology and sociology of the workforce

2 | Understanding Kanban Maturity Levels

The Kanban Maturity Model features seven levels, numbered 0 through 6. For consistency and ease of adoption by technology organizations already familiar with CMMI, levels 1 through 5 are aligned to the five levels of CMMI, with a slight difference in the naming of maturity levels 1, 2, and 3. We have found it useful to extend the model above and below these five stages. The additional levels are inspired by Jerry Weinberg's maturity model from his *Quality Software Management, Volume 1: Systems Thinking*[6].

Level 0 is introduced to model individuals and organizations that are simply oblivious to the need for a process or managerial method. We observe such nascent, immature businesses in our case-study literature. They come to us when they have the epiphany that if their business is to survive and thrive, they do need a process, often choosing Kanban as a means to some management oversight with very little process overhead. Kanban provides some constraints without constraining the emergence of processes and workflows specific to their business.

Level 6 is introduced to provide for double-loop learning where an organization is questioning, Who are we? Is our identity still appropriate? and if not, Who do we want to be? How should we reinvent ourselves? What is our purpose to exist, and is it still relevant? Is our strategy appropriate? Do we offer the correct products and services? Are we choosing to serve the correct market segments, or do they need to change? How should we evaluate and identify market segments to target? Which existing segments should we drop?

We feel that this seven-level model offers a considerable advance and innovation over previous organizational maturity models, while maintaining continuity with models that have preceded it. We believe that our new model will better serve the pursuit of excellence in product and service delivery and encourage behavior for adaptability and long term survival of businesses. The following chapters describe each level in detail.

Maturity Level 0 – Oblivious

At maturity level 0, individuals are responsible for handling their own tasks. Frequently, the person who performs the work is the user of its outcome as well; that is, the work is self-generated tasks rather than customer requested work orders.

Observable behavior

The organization is oblivious to the need to follow a process. There is ambivalence about the value of management or organizational processes or policies. There is no collaborative working or, if there is, there is no recognition of collaboration. Collaboration may be fleeting, on an ad hoc basis without recognition of a pattern or repeated need. There is no concept of "a team"—a group of people who work collaboratively to deliver on a common goal.

The quality and consistency of work done, or services performed, is entirely associated with individuals and their capabilities, skills, experience, and judgment. The organization, and its performance, is extremely fragile to changes in personnel.

There is no instrumentation, as there is no defined process to instrument. Metrics and measures are not present.

Decision making tends to be reactive, emotional, spontaneous, and sometimes difficult to explain.

Observable Kanban patterns

At maturity level 0, the focus is completely on handling personal tasks. Therefore, the observed Kanban patterns include three main types of Personal Kanban[2] boards, used primarily to visualize tasks. The designs observed reflect a growing level of personal maturity and capability at self-management. There is an intention to achieve a level of self-improvement using reflection, and often a cadence emerges as the use of personal kanban becomes habitual (Figure 1).

A *trivial* personal kanban visualizes invisible work, relieving the user of the burden of carrying the list of open tasks in their head. A *simple* personal kanban introduces WIP limits and recognizes a limit to human capacity, a desire for relief from overburdening, and a belief that multitasking causes individual tasks to take longer and their completion to be unpredictable. This second level could be described as a result of the epiphany that it is better to "stop starting, and start finishing." The consequence is a feeling of personal achievement. The *true* personal kanban emerges when individuals realize that there is an existential overhead to a large backlog of unstarted tasks. This third, more mature design includes the act of personal commitment to items that will be done next, while there is recognition that backlog items are actually uncommitted, remain optional, and may be discarded. There is often a cadence to the personal reflection needed to select that which

---

2. Personal Kanban is a registered trademark of Modus Cooperandi, Inc.

will come next. A personal triage capability develops to decide what will be done: now; later, and if later, then roughly when, based on a sense of urgency of the task; or not at all.

From an organizational maturity perspective, this third style of board is still a maturity level 0 (ML0) pattern; however, it reflects the thinking and actions of a more mature individual likely to want to participate in a more mature organization.

Maturity Level 1 – Emerging

At maturity level 1, there is recognition that management adds value and that some organizational structure and transparency to how work is done will offer consistency. **Emerging** covers a wide range of aspects of process, management concepts, and behavior. At the lowest level, there would be no definition of processes, procedures, or workflows. However, some collaborative work will be happening. There is some form of "value-stream" rather than mere individual craft work taking place.

As maturity grows, some initial definition of process workflows, management policies, and decision frameworks emerge. Process definition is "emerging." However, processes, workflows, and policies are not followed consistently and the use of decision frameworks is also inconsistent.

Observable behavior

There is no consistency of process, policy usage, or decision frameworks. There is no

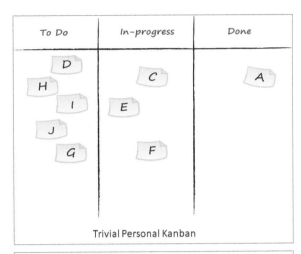

Trivial Personal Kanban

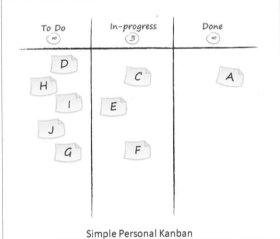

Simple Personal Kanban

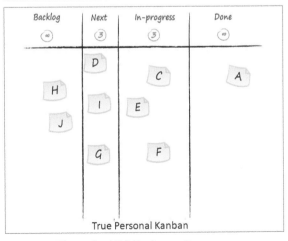

True Personal Kanban

Figure 1   ML0 Kanban patterns

consistency of desired outcome. Work is not seen as a combination of services, and customers perceive service delivery as unreliable.

There is an understanding of what the work is, but perhaps not how it should be done, what the finished product should look like, or the service delivery expectations of customers. There is little understanding of who the customer is or why they have requested the work. Consequently, there is an observable lack of alignment among teams. This affects the consistency of product design and implementation as well as service delivery.

Work is pushed into the process. Priority is set based on superstition, or political leverage, or is purely ad hoc and random. The process, system, or value stream is overloaded. Individuals are often overburdened. There is no concept of a capability or a capacity to the system. Hence, it is impossible to try to balance demand against capability. There is an expectation that everything requested will be done. There is no triage capability or opportunity to refuse work.

Analogously, if we were in the pizza delivery business, we would observe that the method of preparing, baking, and delivering pizza was inconsistent and that defined procedures were not followed consistently. We would also observe that often the pizza delivered was of the wrong type, missing ingredients, or of poor quality upon delivery; or that the delivery time varied dramatically. The customer experience would be to conclude that the vendor is extremely unreliable.

The workplace is stressful because of the inconsistency and poor quality, and there are significant amounts of rework. There is constant pressure to find new customers because existing customers, reacting to the unreliable service, fail to return.

There is considerable luck attached to whether a product or service is "fit-for-purpose." There is a reliance on individual heroics.

Collaboration and the concept of teams is recognized. However, organizational capability and performance is extremely fragile and there is a tendency to rely upon and reward heroic effort and heroic individuals. Customers with sufficient transparency will show a preference or demand the involvement of specific individuals on their work requests as a means to mitigate risks of inconsistent, poor performance and disappointment.

It is highly likely there is loss of discipline when under stress and handling exceptional circumstances. When stressed, the organizational maturity is likely to slip back to level 0, and the organization relies entirely on individual heroics to pull out of the crisis.

Some metrics may be present, though these tend to be focused on individuals rather than on instrumenting still emerging and inconsistently followed processes. There is a tendency to collect and report that which is easy to measure and there is little thought as to whether the measure is useful or actionable. Some local activity measures may serve as general health indicators, though many may be of little actionable value and are essentially vanity metrics—they make a team or its individual members feel good, feel as if they are making progress, but they serve no meaningful purpose in improving business outcomes.

Decision making is emotionally driven and superstitious in nature.

Observable Kanban patterns

At the transition to the level 1 stage, several individuals are working on a common function, but assignments are separated. There may be specialization of tasks to individuals with specific skills. Everyone is responsible for organizing and performing their own tasks, or tasks are assigned and dispatched by a supervisor.

An aggregated personal kanban board (Figure 2) is used to visualize all the tasks and their status for a department or function, typically using one lane per person. Hence, each lane is a personal kanban board, and displayed together they are aggregated. This design often facilitates the "supervisor as dispatcher" who assigns tasks to individuals. However, having awareness of what the other people do and with which work they may require assistance, fosters collaboration. It is the first step to creating a team and developing the understanding that working jointly produces better results more efficiently than working in isolation with limited comprehension of how one's work affects others.

At the core stage of maturity level 1, collaboration happens habitually in a small team performing work with a shared goal or shared responsibility and accountability. Pools of people with different specializations may exist. Each team member is still responsible for

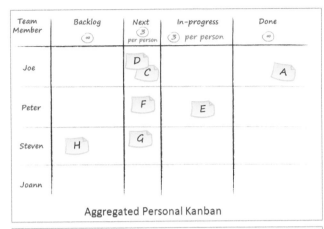

Aggregated Personal Kanban

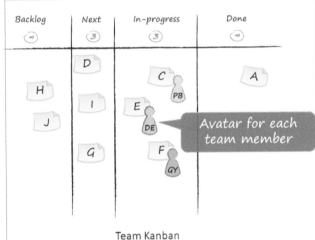

Team Kanban

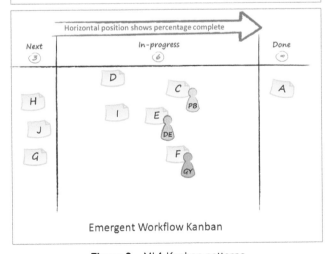

Emergent Workflow Kanban

Figure 2   ML1 Kanban patterns

handling their own tasks; however, the team has an emerging comprehension of the overall development process, in particular how it begins and ends. This lays the foundation for maturity level 2, at which teams start seeing their jobs as a service conducted in response to a customer request or as a part of a larger workflow. Therefore, maturity level 1 is fundamental for making Kanban Service Delivery principles one and two work:

1. Understand and focus on your customer needs and expectations.

2. Manage the work, let people organize around it.

The team visualizes its work and meets daily to check its status. However, the process is not consistent yet, and under stress it is likely to lose discipline and consistency. Performance depends almost totally on the availability and individual efforts of the team members and varies as widely as the spread in individual capabilities across the team.

Maturity Level 2 – Defined

At maturity level 2, there is a basic definition of processes, workflow, policies, and decision frameworks. These are followed consistently. There is recognition that the process definitions describe "the way we do things." However, there is still a lack of consistency in the desired outcome. Customers will observe unacceptable inconsistencies in quality and service delivery, though less so than at maturity level 1.

Observable behavior

The process, policy usage, and decision frameworks are consistent. However, there is still no consistency of the desired outcome.

There is an understanding of what the work is, and both how it should be done and what the finished product should look like, as well as the service delivery expectations. There may not be a full understanding of who the customer is or why they have requested the work. This is most often true for shared and internal services that lack visibility to the end customer and the motivation or purpose behind a work request or the risks associated with that work or its delivery. As a consequence, there may be an observable lack of alignment among teams and interdependent service workflows. This affects the consistency of service delivery as seen by the customer.

A basic understanding and definition of the workflow is developed. Nevertheless, work tends to be pushed into the process because policies are not strong enough or sufficiently internalized as to prevent it. There is little observable capability to prioritize work. Priority, if it exists, may be superstitious, political, or simplistic, such as first-in-first-out. The process, system, or value stream tends to be overburdened. There is a tendency to say "yes" to everything or too many things and an inability to balance demand against capability.

If we were in the pizza delivery business, we would observe that the method of preparing, baking, and delivering pizza was consistent and that defined procedures were now followed consistently. However, we would still observe that the pizza delivered was occasionally of the wrong type, missing ingredients, or of poor quality upon delivery; or that the delivery time differed dramatically from expectations. The customer's perception still would be that the vendor is unreliable.

There is increased collaboration that now spans across teams and facilitates workflow.

The workplace is notably less stressful because of the consistency of process and defined roles and responsibilities. Workers know what is expected of them and what they can expect of their colleagues. Poor quality is still an issue, though less so than at level 1, and there is still some rework. There is still some pressure to find new customers because some existing customers fail to return as a reaction to the unreliable service.

The product or service is often not completely "fit-for-purpose." There is a reliance on line-level managerial heroics to ensure consistency and the meeting of expectations. There is a tendency to reward and venerate heroic managers.

Organizational capability and performance remains fragile. Customers may demand the involvement of specific managers, whom they trust, to mitigate risks of inconsistent, poor performance and disappointment.

There is some tendency to lose discipline when under stress and handling exceptional circumstances. When stressed, the organizational maturity tends to slip back to level 1.

There is rudimentary instrumentation of the defined process. There may be a tendency to measure and report that which can be seen or is easy to instrument. There is little or no alignment of reported metrics with customer expectations. Metrics and measures tend to be locally focused on performing the work, such as cycle times or throughput rates on specific activities or value-adding steps. Most measures are general health indicators, though some may be of little actionable value and should be seen as vanity metrics.

Decision making is usually qualitative in nature or emotionally driven.

Observable Kanban patterns

The main characteristics of the transition from the Emerging to the Defined maturity level is the usage of the Defined workflow with per-person WIP limits on the kanban board (Figure 3). Here, a sequence of the main workflow phases substitute for the generic *In-progress* column of team kanban boards. The types of work are identified and visualized by different colors (in this example) or by different lanes across the board.

The team begins to understand that their performance depends on the amount of work-in-progress; that is, the more work-in-progress, the longer work takes and the less predictable its completion. There is recognition that work left unfinished in a waiting state is not helpful and can lead to much higher defect rates and increased rework.

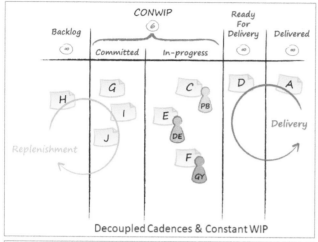

Decoupled Cadences & Constant WIP

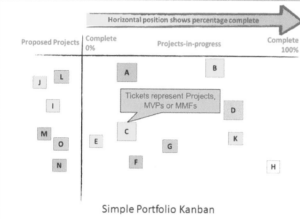

Simple Portfolio Kanban

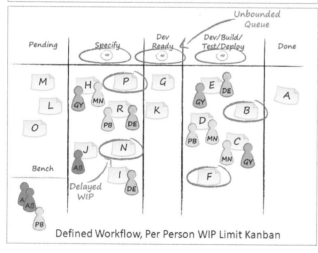

Defined Workflow, Per Person WIP Limit Kanban

Figure 3 ML2 Kanban patterns

Nevertheless, teams using delivery kanban boards with per-person WIP limits deliver better quality results and feel relief from overburdening.

Although the workflow is still basic and the overall process is not consistent at the transition stage, there is emergence of customer focus. There is an understanding that work flows through a series of steps toward completion of something of customer value. It is realized that smooth flow of work is a desirable state for relief from unevenness. Unevenness in arrival of work creates temporary periods of overburdening. Unevenness in flow makes predictable delivery challenging and has a direct effect on customer satisfaction. There is growing appreciation and awareness of more of the Kanban Method's values, but values such as "customer focus" and "balance" are not yet fully embraced and the cultural focus remains inward—"who we are" and "what's in it for us." Improvements are justified on selfish grounds at the team level. There isn't yet an outward-looking altruism or a focus on contributing for the benefit of customers and other stakeholders.

The need to properly coordinate the teamwork (mainly among different specializations) appears to avoid peaks and troughs of workload.

At the core stage of maturity level 2, organizations are better able to coordinate activities with different audiences and decouple the cadences of planning, committing, or selecting work from the cadence of delivery. This reduces the effect of losing rhythm due to concentrating team effort on packaging and handing over completed work and then restarting development. In addition, developing the ability to allow work to be in-progress while a delivery is being made requires strengthening other technical capabilities such as configuration management. Hence, decoupling the rhythm of planning, commitment, doing, and delivering creates positive stress to improve specific enabling practices such as configuration management.

Some teams recognize the need to control the workflow and do it by using a delivery kanban board with a defined commitment point and constant WIP (CONWIP), which is a true pull system, but without a defined workflow. Basic policies for prioritizing, committing work, and visualizing work status are established. Parameters like *% Complete* are introduced and are used to provide additional information about project status and track its conformance to plan. Portfolio kanban boards are used for visualizing the status of multiple projects and making relevant decisions.

Nevertheless, the workflow management responsibility is not explicitly defined. Even in organizations with established project management processes, project managers' duties include planning, monitoring, and controlling project activities against plan but not managing the workflow. There is no one playing the service delivery manager (SDM) role. In some organizations, we've observed the emergence of a "flow manager" role at maturity level 2. This role tends to have an internal focus, actively managing flow for its benefit of relieving temporary overburdening due to unevenness.

At this level, established policies and workflow controls do not enable managing unforeseen events. This is because the feedback from the system is insufficient. Behavior is entirely reactionary. As a consequence, unforeseen events caused by the occurrence of specific risks or more complex situations, for which there is no specific guidance on how to handle them, can take a project or a service out of control. The result is a failure to meet expectations and, often, a regression in observed maturity level to a more individualistic, heroic culture.

Maturity Level 3 – Managed

At maturity level 3, there is an agreed and understood definition of processes, workflow, policies, and decision frameworks. These are followed consistently, and, in addition, desired outcomes are achieved consistently within customer expectations and tolerances.

Observable behavior

There is a consistency of process, policy usage, or decision frameworks. There is now a consistency of desired outcome. Customer expectations are being met. Product design, quality, and service delivery are all within customer expectations and tolerance levels.

There is an understanding of what the work is—both in how it should be done and what the finished product should look like—as well as the service delivery expectations.

There is a strong sense of unity and purpose along the value stream or across the workflow. There is a sense of a team collaborating to deliver a piece of work. There is a full understanding of who the customer is and why they have requested the work. There is a strong sense of fulfilment amongst the workers when delivering finished work.

There is an observable triage capability to prioritize work into three categories: (1) do it now; (2) leave it until later, comprehending when is ideal; (3) discard, reject, do not do it. Demand is balanced against capability and the system is relieved of over-burdening.

If we were in the pizza delivery business, we would observe that the method of preparing, baking, and delivering pizza was consistent and that defined procedures are followed consistently. Pizza is delivered consistently, correctly to request with high quality, and within service delivery expectations. The customer perception is that the vendor is very reliable.

The workplace runs very smoothly under both normal and exceptional circumstances. There is little tendency to panic under stress. There is a strong sense of process, roles, and responsibilities, and workers know how to react to unusual or exceptional circumstances. There is little urgency to find new customers because existing customers provide steady demand.

The product or service is now completely "fit-for-purpose." There is now an absence of heroics. Instead there is reliance on defined methods, processes, and decision frameworks. When things don't go as planned there is action taken to revise methods and procedures rather than blame individuals.

Organizational capability and performance is now resilient. Customers now trust that work is done consistently and there are no specific requests for individual personnel or specific managers.

The organization is now thinking explicitly about services from an external customer-facing perspective. The notion that the organization consists of a network of interdependent services is starting to emerge. There is some recognition of the power and efficiency of effective shared services.

The process is instrumented to collect and report customer fitness criteria metrics. There may be improvement driver metrics present and actively in use. Metrics and measures tend to be end-to-end, with only specific improvement drivers focused on local activities or value-adding steps. There is a clear metrics and reporting strategy with fitness criteria, improvement drivers, and general health indicators being used appropriately. Presence of vanity metrics is unusual and may exist for cultural reasons, or may be explained as evolutionary relics to which there is an emotional attachment and the conditions needed to successfully remove them have not yet materialized.

Despite the considerable instrumentation and availability of metrics, decision making remains mostly qualitative or emotionally driven.

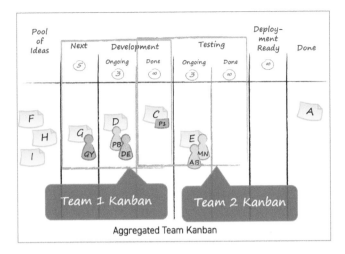

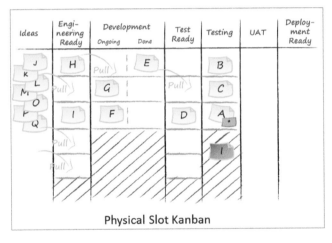

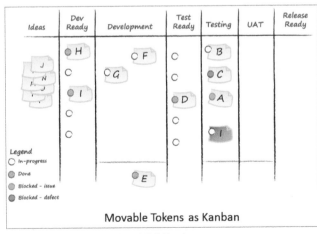

Figure 4a ML3 Kanban patterns

Observable Kanban patterns

A key characteristic of a maturity level 3 transition organization is the usage of kanban systems that visualize a service-oriented, customer-focused workflow. An aggregated team kanban board is used to visualize workflow across different teams (Figures 4a and 4b).

Pull criteria, work item dependencies, defect/rework, and blocked work items are consistently visualized. This facilitates the deeper understanding of the system that performs the work. Initial actions for stabilizing the workflow are in place, in particular, establishing WIP limits for different states and for the entire system, as well as through plotting and interpreting the Cumulative Flow Diagram.

Replenishment Meetings are held to move work items over the commitment point and control the workload to avoid destabilizing the entire system, although the customer might still tend to push starting work in spite of the pull criteria defined by the team.

The processes are repeatable and the teams follow their routines, although they can still abandon them in crisis.

At core stage of ML3, managers and teams have developed a good understanding of the workflow based on experience, collected historic data, and established feedback mechanisms (delivery planning, service delivery, and Risk Reviews). They make decisions using recent information about what is actually happening. In addition, they are able to flexibly manage work in order to effectively deliver expected results. Policies and processes are respected by managers and teams and are followed even in crisis.

The deeper understanding of the workflow allows managing larger and riskier projects with a greater degree of success. Multiple project and service management is in place and dependencies between projects and services are taken into account. Initial Operations Reviews are conducted to understand and address service dependencies.

Higher level management is convinced of the benefits brought by properly managing work. The roles of service request manager and service delivery manager are introduced to ensure correct management both upstream and downstream.

Workflow data is collected and plotted to charts. Although

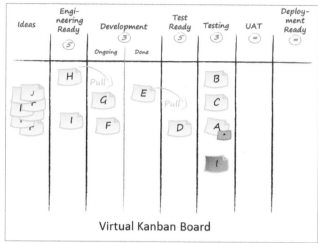

Virtual Kanban Board

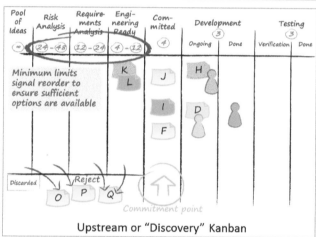

Upstream or "Discovery" Kanban

Figure 4b   ML3 Kanban patterns

data quality is not very good yet and the entire process is not stable enough to produce meaningful measurements, the available data provides information that allows comparing actual and desired project/service state and definition of relevant actions. Analyzing data facilitates the understanding of the processes and starts developing a culture of making decisions based on quantitative information.

Delivery Planning Meetings are held to plan deliveries to customers and to make specific delivery date commitments. The act of committing to doing something is separated from the act of committing to a specific date for delivery. In doing so, customer expectations are better managed and service delivery effectiveness improves. Service Delivery Reviews are conducted to monitor and improve service effectiveness. Risk Reviews are conducted to understand and respond to the risks that impede effective delivery of services.

Maturity Level 4 – Quantitatively Managed

At maturity level 4, design, implementation, and service delivery have become routinely "fit-for-purpose." Consistency of process and consistency of outcome have the effect of relieving a lot of stress, and the organization moves its focus to economic outcomes as well as developing robustness against unforeseen events and exceptional circumstances. Attention is now given to quantitative risk management and economics. The question is now whether consistency of delivery can be achieved within economic expectations of cost or margin, and whether performance can be robust to unforeseen circumstances through appropriate risk hedging. Quantitative analysis of metrics and measures becomes more important. The goal is to be ever "fitter-for-purpose" from the perspective of a variety of stakeholders.

Observable behavior

In addition to all maturity level 3 behaviors, a maturity level 4 organization has a consistent economic performance, such as particular cost targets and margins are being achieved steadily.

Work is now classified by customer risks, and a variety of classes of service is offered. Demand shaping or capacity limitations by work type and class of risk are present. Triage is now driven by risk assessment, and class of service is directly linked to risk. Scheduling is influenced by cost-of-delay and a quantitative understanding of service delivery risks such as the probability distribution of lead time.

If we were in the pizza delivery business, we would now be running an economically successful business offering a number of different classes of service such as an express delivery menu. We successfully cope with ebb and flow in demand and understand the cyclical nature of our business. We are optimally staffed most of the time and our costs are tightly controlled without affecting our delivery capability or impacting customer satisfaction.

Under stress, the organization follows emergency or exception procedures and takes mitigation and remedial action to reduce likelihood and/or impact of occurrence, or completely prevent recurrence.

Organizational capability and performance is now robust. Risk hedging is effective against the occurrence of unforeseen, though not unforeseeable, events. Customers now trust that work is done consistently, and there are no specific customer requests for individual personnel or specific managers. Managers, shareholders, and other stakeholders such as regulatory authorities now trust that work is conducted within defined constraints and that economic outcomes are within a defined range of expectations.

There is extensive systems thinking and service-orientation present in the organization. Organizational units are now forming around defined services with known and understood dependencies. Shared services are recognized as a highly effective and efficient approach and therefore are desirable economically. Shared services are seen as providing an advantage to organizational agility—the ability to reconfigure quickly to changing market, regulatory, or political conditions.

There is a notable shift to quantitative decision making, and a cultural norm is established that decisions must be underpinned with solid data, risks assessed, and adequately hedged prior to action.

Observable Kanban patterns

Maturity level 4 is realized more through use of metrics and feedback loops. It is characterized more by adoption of Kanban Cadences and adoption of the Fit-For-Purpose Framework than specific kanban board designs. However, an organization that is solidly at ML4 visualizes and successfully manages different services and classes of services using shared resources. Capacity is allocated to each service so as to respond to a particular organization's goal or strategy. In addition, capacity allocation is used flexibly as a risk-hedging mechanism against a fluctuating or unpredictable arrival of unplanned work (Figure 5).

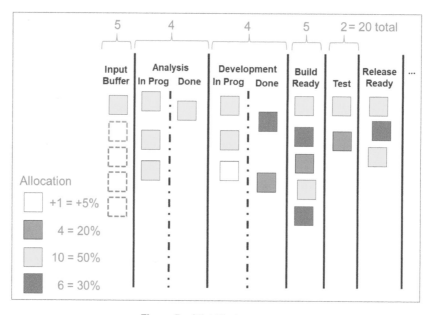

Figure 5   ML4 Kanban patterns

Maturity Level 5 – Optimizing

At maturity level 5, not only have design, implementation, and service delivery become routinely "fit-for-purpose," the business is now entirely "fit-for-purpose" from a shareholder's perspective. The focus is now on optimizing for efficiency and improved economic outcomes, increasing productivity without sacrificing quality, increasing margins, extracting premium prices for premium classes of service or quality, minimizing costs, and optimizing the value of work done through a superior prioritization and triage capability. The goal at ML5 is to be "fittest-for-purpose." A strong culture of continuous improvement has emerged and we observe acts of leadership at all levels contributing to improved performance. The workforce feels empowered to suggest and implement changes. Workers have a sense of ownership over their own processes and a sense of pride in their capabilities and outcomes. There is a culture of "seeking forgiveness" rather than "asking permission" and consequently the organization is able to act and move quickly. Individual units can act with autonomy while remaining aligned to strategy, goals, and objectives. The organization has agility and is readily reconfigured to offer new services and/or classes of service. The business is now solidly robust to changing customer expectations and other externalities.

Observable behavior

At level 5 we see all the observable behavior we associate with levels 3 and 4, and in addition we see a strong *kaizen* culture—an organizational focus on improvement, with feedback mechanisms aimed at optimizing performance.

There is extensive process instrumentation. Improvement opportunities are aligned to customer fitness criteria metrics. Improvement driver metrics are formally established. Improvement drivers have achievable targets. Improvement initiatives are predictive, model-driven, and there is a known causation between improvement action and forecasted outcome. Significant job satisfaction is now derived from delivering improvements, as delivering customer requested work within expectations and to the customer's satisfaction is now routine and is taken for granted.

Economic performance is improving consistently. Process improvement is used as a competitive weapon and an enabler of new services, new classes of service, new markets, and new market segments. Competitors are being outmaneuvered by superior organizational agility, enabling new and better products and services faster than ever.

New services can be rapidly defined and composed of calls to a network of existing shared services. Reconfiguring the organization to serve different markets with different classes of service is now a routine action causing little to no disruption.

Observable Kanban patterns

Maturity level 5 is most definitely characterized by behavior: the use of models, quantitative analysis, extensive use of feedback mechanisms—with most or all of the Kanban Cadences present—and perhaps augmented by additional feedback mechanisms for product management and integration of other evolutionary change methods such as Lean Startup, A3 Thinking, Toyota Kata, or Theory of Constraints. Innovative visualization at ML5 tends to focus on advanced risk management techniques, or the use of simpler kanban boards to visualize and manage improvement initiatives, or the use of additional work item types and capacity allocation for improvement opportunities (sometimes called *kaizen* events).

Across a set of aggregated services, it is possible to visualize fixed or permanently allocated personnel or teams versus floating personnel who can be quickly assigned to assist on any service.

In Figure 6, permanently assigned fixed team members have their names displayed on rows of the board allocated for specific services. At the same time, more generalist, cross-trained personnel are visualized using avatars with their initials. The avatars can be moved from row to row to help where their skills are most needed at any given time.

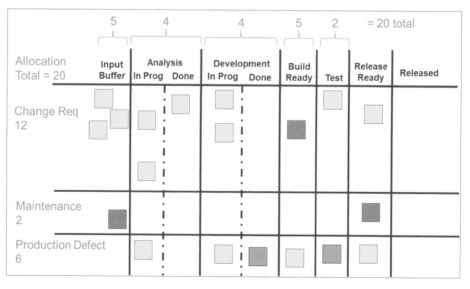

Figure 6   Staff liquidity visualization

Maturity Level 6 – Congruent

Maturity level 6 is when we can claim that a business is truly "built to last." At level 6, we observe several double-loop learning capabilities. The business is capable of questioning:

- Is the way we do things still competitive? Are new technologies, processes, methods, or means becoming available that we should be investigating or adopting?

- Do we offer the right products and services? and if not, how should we change?

- Are we serving the right markets? and do we have the capability to serve our chosen markets adequately?

- Who are we as a company? and is our current identity relevant and appropriate? or do we need to reinvent ourselves?

These would correctly be characterized as strategic concerns, and defining the answers to these questions is a key part of strategic planning. Although the ability to challenge some of these four areas (the use of "double-loop learning") may be observed at shallower maturity levels, a level 6 organization can challenge all four—how, what, why, and who. A level 6 organization not only has the capability to do this strategic planning work but it will also exhibit alignment of capability and service provision with that strategy. When the strategy needs to change, the organization will quickly reconfigure to align with the changes. This concept of strategy being continually aligned to operational capabilities is referred to as "congruent action." Congruent action is leadership that everyone can believe in. A congruent organization is set up for success. Such an organization is extremely robust to changing externalities, including disruptive, discontinuous innovation, and hence will not only exhibit longevity but will absorb dramatic changes to its strategy relatively easily without significant impact in economic performance.

Anticipated behavior

At level 6 we should see all the observable behaviors we associate with level 5. In addition, we should see a strong strategic planning capability and the use of strategic planning reviews questioning current market segmentation, questioning product and service mix, comparing observed capability with strategy, and defining a strategy against which the organization is capable of successfully delivering.

There should be extensive market instrumentation to provide feedback on whether the firm's products and services are viewed as "fit-for-purpose." Market segments should be oriented around customer purpose. The entire business should be service oriented and driven by service delivery. There should be assessment of design, implementation, and service delivery capabilities against expectations in each market segment. The organization should be capable of transparently reporting its fitness-for-purpose in each segment. Improvement actions should be driven by a desire to amplify a segment or switch it off.

There should be a strong sense of identity and an institutionalized understanding of "who we are" as a business and how that affects decision making. However, while identity is well understood, there shouldn't be a dogmatic, blind attachment to it. There should be a recognized willingness to evolve and move with the times. Senior leaders should understand their role as social engineers in defining and managing the identity of the business and its workforce as a social group. Defining and actively managing the culture of the firm should be recognized as the main task of senior leaders. Identity management should be an organizational capability. Tangible actions to manage the identity of the business and the sociology of the workforce should be observable.

3 | Benefits

Developing Organizational Agility and Adaptability

Relief from over-burdening

Implementing Kanban at maturity levels 0 through 2 provides differing levels of relief from overburdening. At level 0, the focus is entirely on the individual. A personal kanban board provides individuals with a limit on their current work and the opportunity to relieve them of too much work-in-progress. This results in happier individuals who take a pride in their work, and focus on finishing, with high quality, tasks that they have started. Tasks are completed faster with greater predictability, and rework is reduced. There is little to no concept of service delivery, and the customer experience is that service delivery is unfit-for-purpose.

At level 1, the scale grows to a team level, and there is the opportunity to relieve a team of too much work-in-progress. This results in happier teams who take a pride in collaborative work, and focus on finishing, with high quality, tasks that they have started. Tasks are completed faster with greater predictability, and rework is reduced. The customer experience remains that service delivery is unfit-for-purpose.

At level 2, an understanding of a service delivery workflow, or value stream, emerges. Each team or individual in the workflow is locally relieved of overburdening, but the whole system may still be overwhelmed with work, and queues or buffers between value-adding functions may be extensive. Queuing discipline is often ad hoc or non-deterministic and, as a consequence, although individuals and teams do better and higher quality work faster with less rework, the entire system fails to exhibit predictability. From an external perspective, maturity level 2 offers few more additional benefits than level 1. From an internal perspective, a greater number of teams are happier, completing more work with a greater pride of workmanship and motivation to improve further.

At maturity levels 0 through 2, local cycle times may be reduced, but the customer's experience of lead time and predictability is that things take too long, and lead time has too much variability. The customer's experience is that service delivery is unpredictable and remains unfit-for-purpose for some or most of the time—less so at ML2 than at ML1 or ML0. The customer may show sympathy toward an improving level of service delivery, while overall, service levels remain unsatisfactory.

Predictability and Faster, Smoother Flow

At maturity level 3, an end-to-end workflow, value stream, or system is now relieved of overburdening. Queues or buffers between value-adding steps are greatly reduced in size, and queuing discipline, defined by classes of service, is emerging. As a consequence, lead times are reduced dramatically, and the variation, or tail, in the lead time distribution function is reduced greatly. The customer experience is faster service with greater predictability. At level 3, customers are likely to start reporting that service delivery is fit-for-purpose.

Organizational Agility

At maturity level 4, the organization has a firm grasp of systems thinking and views itself as a network of interdependent services—a system of systems. Each service may have implemented a kanban system.

The effect is that work with complex dependencies can be delivered efficiently, with little delay as a consequence of interdependent work orders across the network. There is a high level of predictability, even for work with complex dependencies. The customer experience is that, even for large, complex work requests, the service delivery is fit-for-purpose.

By using a service-oriented organizational paradigm, the business can quickly reconfigure shared services to provide new end-to-end service delivery workflows with a minimum of disruption to existing services, personnel, and their roles and responsibilities. The customer experience is the conclusion that time to market, or time to set up and provide new services, is dramatically reduced.

Risk Management and Improved Economic Performance

Also at maturity level 4, the economic performance of the business improves dramatically. Both better governance and appropriate risk hedging improve revenues, margins, and cost control. Demand shaping, capacity allocation, advanced forms of classes of service, risk assessment techniques, and a strong triage function that separates work into three categories—do it now; leave until later, but with a specific schedule; or choose not to do it all—all contribute to highly predictable outcomes and superior economic results.

At maturity level 5, a continuous improvement culture and the use of quantitative analysis of system capability metrics contribute to ever-improving economic results without a loss of customer satisfaction or fitness-for-purpose.

Long-Term Survivability

Maturity levels 1 through 5 provide various scales of single-loop learning—getting better at what we do and how we do it. Maturity level 6 sees the emergence of two forms of double-loop learning. This manifests as a capability to question:

- Is our strategy correct? Are we offering the right products and services to the right markets? Should we redefine our market segmentation and change the products and services we offer?

and

- Do we as a business have the right identity for the current business, political, economic, and technological environments in which we compete?

A level 6 organization is capable of both questioning its own identity and reinventing itself in a new image, with a new identity.

Although the elements of double-loop learning that manifest in Kanban, with practices such as Strategy Review, may emerge at lower levels, their effectiveness is diminished through a lower maturity of the rest of the organization. For example, what is the point of defining new markets and new services to offer if the organization is not capable of reconfiguring itself to offer them in a timely and effective manner? What is the point of targeting new market segments if the organization is not capable of meeting the product specification, quality, or service delivery expectations of customers in that segment? What is the point of targeting new markets with new products if the organization cannot guarantee to exploit them profitably? Lower levels of maturity might enable level 6. But, put simply, implementing level 6 practices in a level 2 organization is likely to be ineffective, and it might result in disappointment, finger-pointing, and assigning blame for failure.

Maturity level 6 organizations are robust to rapidly changing external environments. They are capable of reacting quickly and effectively to disruptive, discontinuous technological innovation, changes in the regulatory environment, changes in the political or economic climate, changes in customer tastes, or raised customer expectations.

Establishing Shared Purpose

The culture of an organization has a direct relationship to the ability to achieve a given level of maturity and maintain it consistently. To effectively reach high levels of maturity, senior leaders must view part of their role as that of social engineers. If a leader desires the benefits of higher maturity levels, then it is her or his job to lead and steer the culture such that higher maturity is achievable.

Lower maturity organizations at levels 0 through 2 tend to have an individualistic focus on their identity or their culture: who am I? and what's in it for me? Or at a team level, who are we? and what's in it for us? There can be selfishness in low maturity organizations, or in the workers and their teams. Individuals, teams, or the whole organization may cast themselves as victims, with a culture of shared affinity as victims, powerless to affect their circumstances or break free from an abusive environment. Alternatively, lower maturity organizations are nascent, emerging and perhaps working in nascent or emergent markets. They are still finding themselves, defining who they are and why they exist. With enough time and leadership, they might mature to level 3 or beyond.

Low maturity organizations are often highly socially cohesive, and conformance to social norms and established tribal behaviors tends to drive decision making and outcomes. Consequently, there is considerable inertia against change. In highly socially cohesive cultures, change must come from the top. Leaders must signal changes and give permission for them to happen. They must communicate a change in "how we see ourselves"—the self-image and identity of the organization—and perhaps a change in "what we value"—the organizational values. Dependence on a single strong leader implies fragility.

At maturity level 3, an organization has a strong sense of "who we are" and is very comfortable with its identity. As such, it is able to focus energy and attention on the more important topic of "why we exist." A level 3 organization has a strong sense of purpose, defined and communicated by its leaders. Pursuit of the purpose is considered culturally more important than "who we are," the collective identity and self-image of the organization. As such, the organization is more flexible, more tolerant, more trusting, and, consequently, more agile through the cultural importance of "why we exist" rather than obsessing over "who we are." Level 3 organizations have *Einheit*—unity and alignment behind a sense of purpose. Level 3 organizations can act with greater autonomy and exhibit greater agility because of this shared sense of purpose.

At maturity level 4, the organization understands very well "why we exist" and "who we are." The focus now changes to "what we do" in order that we deliver on "why we exist." Selecting the right things to do, to produce the best results, is culturally important to a level 4 organization. They don't just know why they exist, they are good at delivering against that purpose because they select the right products or product features and the right services to best deliver on their goals, and they have a strong and justifiable sense of pride in who they are.

At maturity level 5, the organization has a strong sense of who they are, is comfortable in their skin, knows why they exist, believes in their purpose, and makes good choices to deliver against that purpose effectively in a manner that customers love. This enables them to focus on "how we do it" with a goal of being the best at what they do through superior processes and capabilities.

At maturity level 6, an organization is capable of questioning and changing all of the above. They will question how, what, why, and who. While they have a strong sense of how, what, why and who, these ideas are loosely held. They have cohesion, unity, agreement, and pride in their collective mastery, but they also have a strong culture of challenging established norms and finding better ways. They value challenging established conventions, norms, and behaviors. They value innovation, and they embrace change. This is driven from an overarching value: the desire for longevity, the desire to survive for generations. A level 6 organization recognizes that stubbornness, and a refusal to change their how, or their what, or their why, or even their identity—their self-image, their "who"—may lead to their extinction.

Fostering Organizational Values

The Kanban values [11], identified by Mike Burrows and codified in his book, *Kanban from the Inside* [10], are also mapped against organizational maturity levels.

Table 1   Original Kanban Values

Maturity Level	Value
1	Transparency Collaboration
2	Flow
3 (transitional)	Respect Understanding Agreement Customer Service[*]
3 (core)	Balance Leadership
* Originally documented as "Customer Focus"	

In addition, we found the need to extend the set of values to express those we saw driving behavior enabling Kanban adoption that were not captured in Mike's original set. Each value is also mapped to the organizational maturity level that it enables. The important nuance is that holding the value enables the maturity level. The reverse is unlikely to be true—an organization doesn't strive for a maturity level in order to hold a value. Values come first. Values are drivers. Values are enabling constraints, they enable a maturity level and those beyond it.

Table 2   Extended Kanban Values

Maturity Level	Value
0	Achievement
3	Purpose Regulatory compliance
5	Experimentation
6	Diversity Tolerance

For example, valuing a sense of purpose, and ensuring that it is communicated and understood, is a key enabler of maturity level 3. It is unlikely that maturity level 3 or beyond can be achieved without it.

In addition, we observe the need for explicit business values to drive achievement of deeper maturity. These are governing constraints in that they express the limit of what is possible while holding that value. For example, valuing short-term results without valuing long-term investment tends to limit a business to a maximum of maturity level 4.

Table 3   Business values which drive Kanban maturity

Maturity Level	Business Value
4	Market focus Short-term results
5	Business focus Long-term investment (patient capital)
6	Business survivability

Integration with Capability Maturity Model Integration (CMMI)

CMMI for Development (CMMI-DEV) and CMMI for Services (CMMI-SVC) are two models actively used for defining, managing, and improving processes in product development and service organizations. They help organizations to identify gaps where improving process capability will have the most impact on achieving an organization's goals, keep customers happy, and ensure that work is done as effectively as possible.

KMM is a model for evolving an organization's fitness to meet their purpose. Strongly focused on creating a fast, smooth, and efficient flow of value, it improves transparency and collaboration, reduces overburdening of individuals, and targets predictable delivery on customer expectations. KMM practices develop the sense of unity and purpose of the teams across the workflow. It balances demand and capability of the system and optimizes the value stream and economic outcomes by means of a strong prioritization and triage discipline.

CMMI has five maturity levels (ML) and each level builds on the previous one for continuous improvement. Organizations that work toward higher maturity levels get advanced capabilities and promote more effective processes.

KMM defines seven maturity levels. It extends the CMMI levels with ML0 and ML6. ML0 is about managing an individual's work. ML6 is about developing a congruent business.

The thinking behind CMMI's levels begins with an assumption that work must be contained. Similar to Kanban and KMM, work is already in progress but in CMMI, project and service organizations must understand and contain and define the work first, even before they begin to build out the processes to perform the work. CMMI assumes throughput issues are due to poorly defined expectations, processes, and process control—in that order—and not necessarily due to overloaded people and operations. The target state for organizations using CMMI, therefore, is to work toward high-fidelity organizational processes via steps of increasing process insight and statistical control, beginning with defining the work itself. Underlying assumptions within CMMI are that all matters will be handled at the organizational level. A "high-maturity" CMMI organization will take on new work consistent with its known capabilities—becoming a "center of excellence" for the type of work they do.

KMM, on the other hand, begins with an assumption that organizations and the individuals within them want to befit the work they do. KMM further assumes that lack of understanding of the work is a symptom of too much work—which overshadows everything else, including processes—and leaves no room for improving the situation, understanding the work, or containing it. KMM sees throughput issues as due to lack of insight into or feedback on the work caused by overburdening the people and the operation they work in. The target state for organizations using KMM, therefore, is to work toward full appreciation of the work through a deepening understanding of the organization's capabilities. Underlying assumptions within KMM are that all matters begin and end with the individuals in it. A "high maturity" KMM organization has congruence between themselves and the work, regardless of the nature, and deftly and strategically adapts itself to the work—reflecting the demand from the market.

CMMI maturity level 1 (ML1), Initial, is not explicitly defined. In general, it is understood as not reaching maturity level 2, and that the work isn't managed and the processes surrounding the work are not defined. In KMM ML1 defines the behaviors of an organization that begins developing an understanding of its workflow.

The names of the maturity levels 2 and 3 are interchanged for the following reasons:

- CMMI ML2, Managed, is about establishing the basic project and service management practices around the work to be done. At KMM ML2, an organization develops a basic understanding of the entire workflow, defines relevant policies and decision frameworks, and applies them consistently. Therefore KMM ML2 is named Defined.

- CMMI ML3, Defined, extends the range of established processes as well as their level of institutionalization. At KMM ML3, an organization introduces practices that ensure a consistent workflow, predictability, achieving desired outcomes, and meeting service level agreements efficiently. These are used to manage successfully multiple projects and shared services. Therefore KMM ML3 is called Managed.

KMM complements the CMMI Project Management and Process Management process areas in the following way:

- Project Management:

  o Kanban introduces the service-oriented approach to project management. This implies that project development is seen through a collection of interdependent services; for example, design a feature, develop functionality, test functionality, and so on. Each service has to be appropriately staffed and managed in order to deliver the expected outcome to the next service of the value chain in time.

  o The visual kanban boards facilitate real-time understanding of the current state of projects and services, issues that impede their development and delivery, dependencies on other stakeholders, and risks of delay. The time for obtaining status reports and coordination meetings shrinks significantly.

  o Having a real-time, visual, and shared understanding of the status of the individual projects and services focusses the monitoring and control activities on what affects the value delivery flow and how to resolve the impediments.

  o Communication at a team level becomes fluent once the habit of conducting the Kanban Meetings is established. The visual aspects of the kanban systems and the Kanban Cadences facilitate the communication and alignment of different teams and stakeholders, as well as to different hierarchy levels.

  o Establishing team norms and shared processes, and coordination within and among integrated teams are organic results of using integrated kanban boards.

  o Kanban establishes explicit policies for prioritizing and managing work. Therefore, team members get sufficient autonomy to decide what work to do next. The project manager's job is more involved with resolving blocking issues, ensuring smooth flow between stages, scheduling, and coordinating stakeholders and other teams. The service manager's job includes proper capacity allocation to ensure timely demand processing.

o Instead of using discrete task estimation, in Kanban the delivery date of a work item is forecasted based on historical data of lead time for the corresponding work type as well as by means of Little's Law.

o Kanban uses classes of services that are defined based on understanding the business risks associated to the work items, in particular, their cost of delay.

o Risk evaluation is based on a previous blocker clustering and analysis, which brings a thorough understanding of the impediments for the workflow as well as eliminates the ambiguity of the Probability and Impact parameters.

- Process Management:

o The purpose of improving the flow of valuable work and delivering on customer expectations focusses the process improvement effort on the aspects that are important to the business. This involves eliminating unnecessary over-processing and reducing transaction and coordination costs. In addition, it implies an appropriate integration of individual processes or sub-processes in order to streamline the accomplishment of the expected outcome.

o A positive consequence of this value-driven process improvement is that people understand the need for establishing defined processes and see the value of their continuous improvement. This facilitates their adoption and reduces the effort for managing the change.

o Project-level processes are defined directly on kanban boards. Project-specific performance metrics are supported directly from kanban board data.

o Process performance objectives, at the project, service, and organizational levels are supported directly from kanban data.

Using CMMI and KMM practices together helps product-development and service-delivery organizations to increase process agility and align better business and process objectives.

In addition, Kanban principle "Start with what you do now, respecting current roles and responsibilities" facilitates its adoption and is, in fact, a critical enabling factor for organizations with well-defined hierarchical structures that pursue agility but are not keen on taking a radical change and restructuring.

Integration with Lean/TPS

The Kanban Method is arguably much closer to the Toyota Way management system and its Toyota Production System than Western-authored literature on Lean. Arguably, the Kanban Method is a means to implement the management system and culture of Toyota into professional services, knowledge worker businesses. Lean literature has a tendency to focus on elimination of waste, value-stream mapping, industrial engineers designing out wasteful, non-value-adding steps, and then deploying new processes into organizations using a managed approach to change. Lean, as practiced by American and other Western consulting firms, generally does not replicate the employee-empowered *kaizen* culture of continuous improvement, and it fails to take an evolutionary and incremental approach to change driven by shop-floor workers and line managers. The Kanban Method, by comparison, does achieve this *kaizen* culture, and it replicates the empowered employee-driven approach to change, producing incremental and evolutionary improvement.

Toyota uses three words, which were all translated as "waste" in Western Lean literature: *muda*, meaning non-value-adding; *mura*, meaning unevenness; and *muri*, meaning overburdening. Lean has tended to focus on *muda*—removal or reduction of non-value-adding activities. This was relatively effective in industrial, tangible goods businesses. However, with intangible goods, such as professional services businesses, many roles are not considered value-adding. For example, everything a project manager does would be labelled as non-value-adding. If it is known and understood that Lean consultants have arrived to "eliminate waste," then people in non-value-adding roles become fearful and resistant.

The Kanban Method differentiates itself from Lean by pursuing *muri*, then *mura*—first relieving individuals, teams, and workflows of overburdening, then focusing on a faster, smoother, more even flow. This approach works better with human psychology. First, workers gain the ability to take greater pride in their work, and psychologically they are relieved of the existential overhead of thinking about too many pieces of work that have been started but remain open and incomplete. Second, by improving predictability, customer satisfaction is improved and workers gain a greater sense of purpose and mastery of their work. Workers like to be relieved of overburdening and they like their workload to flow evenly. Workers do not like to be labelled as waste.

The Kanban Maturity Model provides a clear and clean integration with Toyota's system. Maturity levels 0 through 2 are primarily focused on *muri*—relief from overburdening at the individual, team, and workflow levels. Maturity level 3 is focused on *mura*—achieving evenness of flow. Maturity level 4 introduces a focus on *muda* as non-value-adding activities—transaction and coordination costs—are reduced in order to improve economic performance. Maturity level 5 produces a full implementation of *kaizen* culture with enterprise scale, evolutionary improvements being driven from the ground up, in pursuit of ever more fit-for-purpose products and services. Maturity level 6 delivers on effective strategy deployment, or *hoshin kanri*, by providing the means to question the how, what, why and who of the enterprise and through leadership, strategic planning and communication of intent, redefine any or all of these.

Integration with the Real World Risk Model

Nassim Nicholas Taleb introduced a taxonomy for assessing the risk exposure of individuals and corporations with his series of books known collectively as The Incerto: *Fooled by Randomness*; *The Black Swan*; *Antifragile*; and most recently, *Skin in the Game*. Following publication of *Antifragile*, he formed the Real World Risk Institute, based in New York City, with a goal to democratize risk management. For this reason, we've chosen to name Taleb's model the Real World Risk Model as a means to refer to its elements collectively.

Taleb uses four adjectives to define the risk exposure of four types of entity: fragile, resilient, robust, and antifragile.

A fragile entity is so exposed to the occurrence of a relatively probable event that, if the event occurs, the entity will cease to exist or suffer a financial bankruptcy.

A resilient entity lives in an environment with a high probability of an undesirable event which, were it to occur, would inflict a severe blow to the entity. However, it doesn't die as a consequence of the severe blow and is capable of picking itself up, licking itself down, healing its wounds, and recovering.

A robust entity has prepared itself in such a fashion that it expects bad things to happen and when they do, it is sufficiently well prepared that it rebuffs or deflects any damage and carries on relatively undamaged from the impact of the event.

An antifragile entity is one that responds to the stress of undesirable events by changing, adapting, and improving. An antifragile organization strives to be continually fit-for-purpose and has an ability to mutate in response to changing externalities that threaten its existence.

These ideas map to the Kanban Maturity Model as follows:

Organizations at maturity levels 0 through 2 are fragile. They are extremely exposed to risks and have little to no concept of risk nor capability at risk management. They are exposed to single points of failure such as relying on a single leader, manager, or individual contributor who must play the role of hero during periods of stress.

Maturity level 3 organizations have an emerging capability at risk management, primarily focused on trimming the tail of lead time distributions to improve predictability. Level 3 organizations also have a strong sense of purpose. They have unity and alignment behind a sense of purpose. Level 3 organizations have a reason to pick themselves up, shake themselves down, and carry on after the impact of an undesirable event. Level 3 organizations are not exposed to single points of failure, nor do they rely on single individuals for their survival. Level 3 organizations have resilience.

At maturity level 4, the superior capability in quantitative analysis or processes and capabilities, coupled to other qualitative analysis techniques in management of business risks and other externalities enables risk hedging through capacity allocation, demand shaping, class of service provisions, real option pricing, advanced scheduling with dynamic reservation systems, and other capabilities within the Enterprise Services Planning (ESP) body of knowledge. Because level 4 organizations are adequately risk hedged, they are robust. At maturity level 5, the robustness is improved. Level 5 organizations can rebuff bigger impacts through their superior economic performance.

Antifragility, the ability to mutate as a response to stress from the environment, is a level 6 capability. It comes from the feedback loops of Strategy Review and Operations Review and the cultural ability to question how, what, why, and who. Level 6 organizations are capable of reinventing themselves in response to stresses from the market. As such, they have long-term survivability. They are antifragile.

Integration with Mission Command

The Mission Command/Maneuver Warfare/*Auftragstaktik* is a doctrine or system of command (system of giving orders) taught to military officers throughout NATO forces. It is most strongly associated with the US Marine Corps. Mission Command has its origins in the Prussian armies of the 19th Century and was developed to enable armies to move quickly, and in a coordinated fashion, as both the scale increased and the effectiveness of weaponry improved dramatically. Mission Command creates empowerment without loss of control. It enables trust at large scale, and coordination of action from organizational units acting with autonomy.

A key concept in Mission Command is that of *Einheit*, meaning "unity and alignment." The German language term is rooted in the origins of the method with Helmut von Moltke, a key figure in the Prussian military throughout most of the 19th Century. With Kanban, *Einheit* is required to achieve maturity level 3 at any scale larger than a small team. It should be introduced by leaders in maturity level 2 organizations. The *Einheit*, or unity of purpose, should be focused on the customer, their work orders, and their demands and expectations. The Kanban value of Customer Focus is required to provide unity and alignment. Leaders must learn to clearly communicate the goal—to serve the customer better, with a better product, designed better, implemented better, and with better service delivery.

4 | KMM Architecture

Maturity Levels and General Practices

The Kanban Maturity Model architecture has two dimensions:

- Vertical: the seven maturity levels described in Chapter 2.

- Horizontal: the six General Practices of the Kanban Method:

  o Visualize (VZ)

  o Limit Work-in-Progress (LW)

  o Manage flow (MF)

  o Make policies explicit (XP)

  o Implement feedback loops (FL)

  o Improve collaboratively, evolve experimentally (using models and the scientific method) (IE)

We characterize the maturity level as having depth, while the implementation of the General Practices of the Kanban Method is said to bring breadth to the implementation.

Figure 7 provides an overview of the KMM architecture.

Specific Practices

Each of the general practices can be implemented with one or more specific practices. These practices may have varying levels of fidelity, which are generally related to the depth

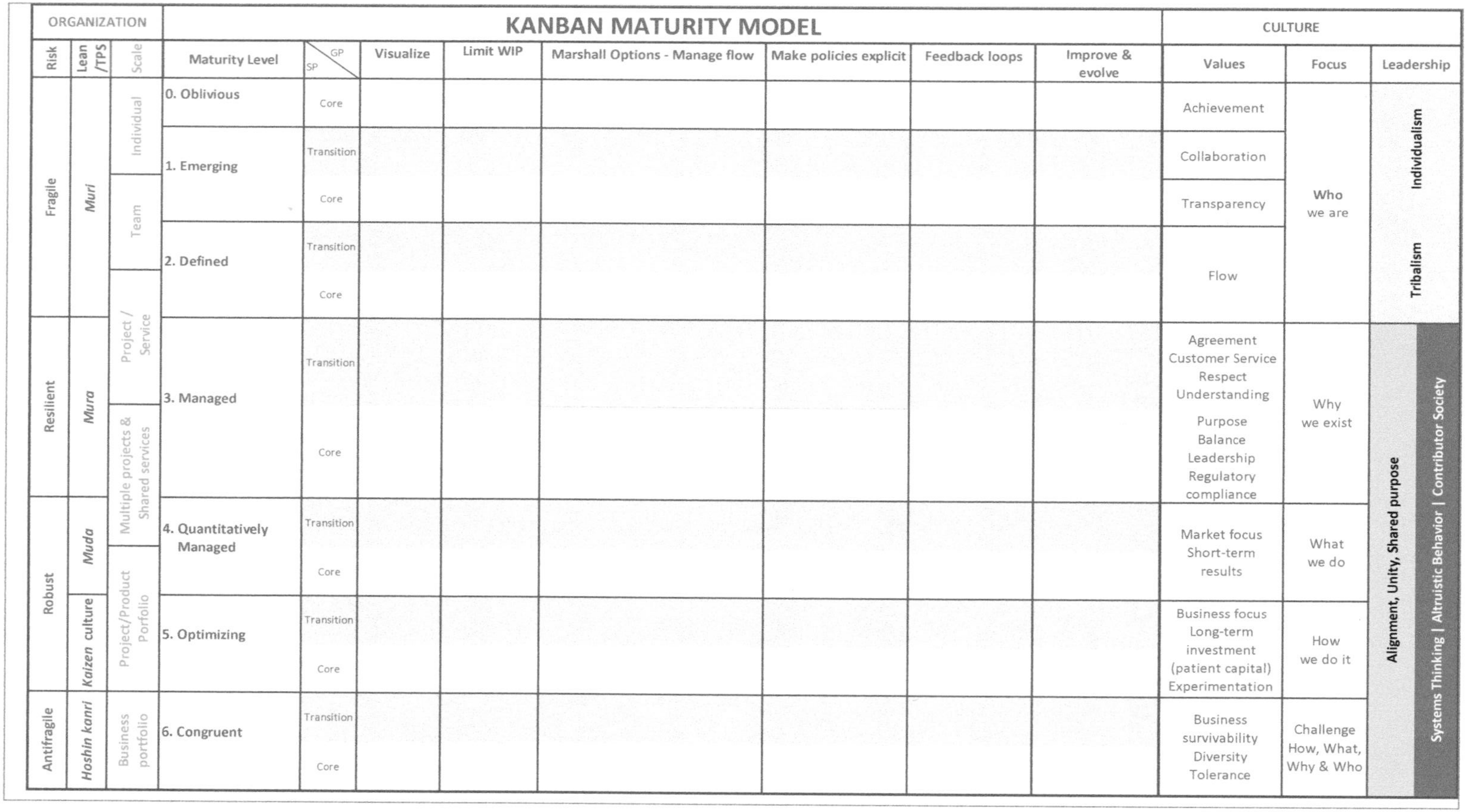

KANBAN MATURITY MODEL

ORGANIZATION

Risk	Lean/TPS	Scale
Fragile	Muri	Individual
Fragile	Muri	Team
Resilient	Mura	Project / Service
Resilient	Mura	Multiple projects & Shared services
Robust	Muda	Project/Product Portfolio
Robust	Kaizen culture	Project/Product Portfolio
Antifragile	Hoshin kanri	Business portfolio

Maturity Level / KMM

Maturity Level	SP/GP	Visualize	Limit WIP	Marshall Options - Manage flow	Make policies explicit	Feedback loops	Improve & evolve
0. Oblivious	Core						
1. Emerging	Transition / Core						
2. Defined	Transition / Core						
3. Managed	Transition / Core						
4. Quantitatively Managed	Transition / Core						
5. Optimizing	Transition / Core						
6. Congruent	Transition / Core						

CULTURE

Values	Focus	Leadership
Achievement	Who we are	Individualism
Collaboration	Who we are	Tribalism
Transparency	Who we are	Tribalism
Flow	Who we are	—
Agreement, Customer Service, Respect, Understanding	Why we exist	Alignment, Unity, Shared purpose
Purpose, Balance, Leadership, Regulatory compliance	Why we exist	Alignment, Unity, Shared purpose
Market focus, Short-term results	What we do	Alignment, Unity, Shared purpose
Business focus, Long-term investment (patient capital), Experimentation	How we do it	Alignment, Unity, Shared purpose
Business survivability, Diversity, Tolerance	Challenge How, What, Why & Who	Systems Thinking | Altruistic Behavior | Contributor Society

Figure 7   KMM architecture

of organizational maturity. Therefore, the name of a specific practice reflects both its fidelity and the depth of maturity of the organization implementing the practice.

For example, **Implement feedback loops** has the following specific practices:

- FL2.1 Conduct internal team Replenishment Meeting at ML2.

- FL3.1 Conduct Replenishment Meeting at ML3.

These are effectively just two versions of the same practice with differing fidelity.

The focus of FL2.1 is internal, and the attendees will tend to be the workers involved in the service delivery workflow or process. The selection of new work is determined by the workers, who pull from some defined backlog.

With FL3.1, the meeting will now include customers, and selection will generally be made by the customers, or by a consensus of all stakeholders present. The purpose of the meeting is the same regardless of implementation, but at the deeper maturity level, there is a recognition that there are customers, they have risks to manage, and they have expectations to be met. By including customers in the system replenishment and enabling them to affect the sequencing and scheduling of work through the system, risk is pushed upstream, to people better informed to manage it appropriately. Hence, risk management is improved, and we recognize that the Replenishment Meeting (FL3.1) is a deeper, more mature variation of an internal team Replenishment Meeting (FL2.1).

The collection of specific practices defined at each maturity level are derived from patterns observed in the field and are associated with organizations exhibiting the behaviors and outcomes associated with a maturity level.

Transition and Core Practices

Specific practices at maturity levels 1 through 6 are organized into two broad groupings:

- Transition practices

- Core practices

When an organization aspires to achieve the outcomes that characterize the next level of maturity, it can add transition practices to facilitate that transition. So long as there is the will and intent to achieve the next level of depth in maturity, these practices should meet with little or no resistance in adoption or implementation.

Core practices are practices that are necessary in order to achieve the outcomes that define a maturity level; however, an organization at the lower level will tend to resist or repel them unless some preparatory work is done first.

The Kanban Maturity Model, with its inclusion of the six General Practices of Kanban—giving the model both breadth and depth—is intended to obviate and replace the Depth of Kanban Assessment Framework first published in 2012 [7].

Architectural Extensions

It is possible to extend the published KMM in two fashions: by mapping additional practices to the existing model and publishing them collectively as a Kanban Maturity Model eXtension (KMMX); and by extending the existing model with additional general practices and then mapping specific practices against these additional general practices and associated maturity levels. Two KMMXs are envisaged, based on the broader Lean Kanban body of knowledge and planned for publication in 2018:

- KMMX for Enterprise Services Planning (ESP)
- KMMX for Leadership

The KMMX for Enterprise Services Planning will map around seventy specific ESP practices against the existing KMM—with each ESP specific practice falling within the scope of an existing general practice of the Kanban Method.

The KMMX for Leadership will map the techniques and practices taught in the Kanban coaching professional curriculum using an additional set of general leadership practices. Specific practices will then be mapped by general leadership practice against specific maturity levels. This will provide guidance on the leadership behaviors needed to move an organization to a given level of Kanban maturity.

It is envisaged that third parties will wish to create their own mappings for other bodies of knowledge and management or process improvement methods. It would be reasonable to suggest that Mission Command, or its close relative OODA (Observe, Orient, Decide, Act), might be mapped as an additional KMMX. Lean Kanban Inc., encourages third parties to create and publish their own extensions demonstrating integration of other methods with Kanban and the KMM.

By providing this extension framework, it is hoped that the core KMM can remain small and its maintenance over the coming years will not be overly burdensome. Full details of how to create and publish official KMMXs will follow later in 2018.

Part II | General and Specific Practices

5 | Visualize

Goals

- To provide individuals, teams, and managers visibility on the work, the workflows, and the risks associated with it
- To engage sensory perception and move people emotionally
- To encourage greater empathy and create greater transparency
- To enable collaboration, better communication, debate, challenge, and catalyze improvement
- To facilitate decision making

Benefits

- Makes that which is invisible, visible
- Ensures clear and correct communication of information about work items
- Reduces overburdening by visualizing and limiting the work-in-progress to the capacity of the individuals that make up the kanban system
- Develops a shared understanding of objectives, work status, impediments, and risks
- Captures significant business risks associated with work items
- Facilitates timely and coherent decision making, collaboration, and knowledge sharing
- Develops trust
- Reduces disruptions

Specific Practices Summary

Maturity Level		Visualization (VZ) Practice
ML0	Core	**VZ0.1** Visualize an individual's work by means of a personal kanban board. **VZ0.2** Visualize basic work item related information on a ticket.
ML1	Transition	**VZ1.1** Visualize work for several individuals by means of an aggregated personal kanban board.
	Core	**VZ1.2** Visualize the work carried out by a team by means of a team kanban board. **VZ1.3** Use avatars to visualize an individual's workload. **VZ1.4** Visualize initial policies. **VZ1.5** Visualize teamwork by means of an emergent workflow kanban board.
ML2	Transition	**VZ2.1** Visualize work items by means of a delivery kanban board with per-person WIP limits. **VZ2.2** Visualize work types by means of card colors or board rows. **VZ2.3** Visualize blocked work items. **VZ2.4** Visualize development of options by means of a discovery kanban board. **VZ2.5** Visualize individual workload on a discovery kanban board by means of per-person WIP limits, potentially implemented using avatars. **VZ2.6** Visualize basic policies.
	Core	**VZ2.7** Ticket design: Visualize concurrent or unordered activities with checkboxes. **VZ2.8** Ticket design: Visualize concurrent activities performed by specialist teams using partial rows. **VZ2.9** Board design: Visualize sequential activities where no dependency or preferred sequence exists using rows or vertical spaces. **VZ2.10** Visualize defects and other rework types. **VZ2.11** Use CONWIP with an emergent workflow delivery kanban board to provide workflow-level relief from overburdening and basic mechanics of a pull system, with separate replenishment and delivery cadences. **VZ2.12** Visualize workflow by means of enhanced discovery/delivery boards. **VZ2.13** Visualize project progress on a portfolio kanban board.

Maturity Level		Visualization (VZ) Practice
ML3	Transition	**VZ3.1** Visualize "ready to commit" status, also known as "ready to pull." **VZ3.2** Visualize "ready to pull" criteria, also known as "definition of ready," or "entry criteria." **VZ3.3** Visualize workflow and teamwork items by means of aggregated team kanban board. **VZ3.4** Visualize project work items on a two-tiered project kanban board. **VZ3.5** Visualize parent–child and peer–peer dependencies. **VZ3.6** Use a parking lot to visualize dependent work requests of another service or system currently waiting or blocked.
	Core	**VZ3.7** Visualize upstream options by means of an upstream/discovery kanban board. **VZ3.8** Visualize discarded options using a bin on an upstream/discovery kanban board. **VZ3.9** Visualize replenishment signals. **VZ3.10** Visualize pull signals. **VZ3.11** Visualize pull criteria (also known as "pull policies," "definition of ready," or "exit criteria"). **VZ3.12** Visualize available capacity. **VZ3.13** Visualize work item aging. **VZ3.14** Visualize target date or SLA. **VZ3.15** Visualize failure demand versus value demand. **VZ3.16** Visualize aborted work. **VZ3.17** Visualize class of service using ticket colors, board rows, or ticket decorators. **VZ3.18** Use Earned Value portfolio kanban board to visualize project progress and schedule or budget risk.
ML4	Transition	**VZ4.1** Visualize local cycle time. **VZ4.2** Use ticket decorators to indicate risks. **VZ4.3** Visualize risk classes with different swim lanes **VZ4.4** Visualize split-and-merge workflows.
	Core	**VZ4.5** Visualize WIP limits on dependencies parking lot. **VZ4.6** Visualize waiting time in dependencies parking lot. **VZ4.7** Visualize SLA exceeded in dependencies parking lot.
ML5	Transition	
	Core	**VZ5.1** Visualize fixed teams and floating workers (shared resources) across aggregated services.

Specific Practices Descriptions

Maturity Level 0

Core practices

VZ0.1 Visualize an individual's work by means of a personal kanban board.

The personal kanban board visualizes an individual's work items and their state (see Figure 8).

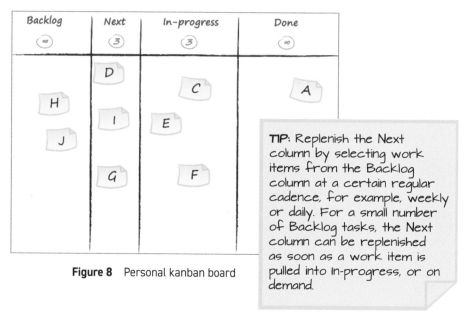

TIP: Replenish the Next column by selecting work items from the Backlog column at a certain regular cadence, for example, weekly or daily. For a small number of Backlog tasks, the Next column can be replenished as soon as a work item is pulled into In-progress, or on demand.

Figure 8   Personal kanban board

Description

- A ticket represents a work item, typically a task.

- Each board column explicitly shows the tasks' state: *Done*, *In-progress* (or currently carrying out), *Next to start*, and *Backlog* (or list of all remaining work). The intent of the Next column is to relieve the person from overburdening because of the number of tasks she has to do, let her focus on those tasks that are In-progress, and complete them without losing time due to multitasking.

- The numbers under the column names specify how many tickets can live in a column at a moment (see LW0.1, page 83).

VZ0.2 Visualize basic work item related information on a ticket.

The information visualized on a ticket has to facilitate quick understanding and decision making about the work to be done.

Description

- Use a kanban card/ticket to represent a work item.

- Summarize key information about the task: title or short summary, due date. Think about the outcome to be developed when defining the title. More detailed information about the tasks can be provided in other systems or in personal notes.

- Further on, for better control of the individual's work, annotate the date (and time, if necessary) when a work item was requested, as well as when real work on it started.

Maturity Level 1

Transition practices

VZ1.1 Visualize work for several individuals by means of an aggregated personal kanban board.

Use the aggregated personal kanban board (Figure 9) to provide visibility to the work carried out by several people. Each person handles her own work items (tasks).

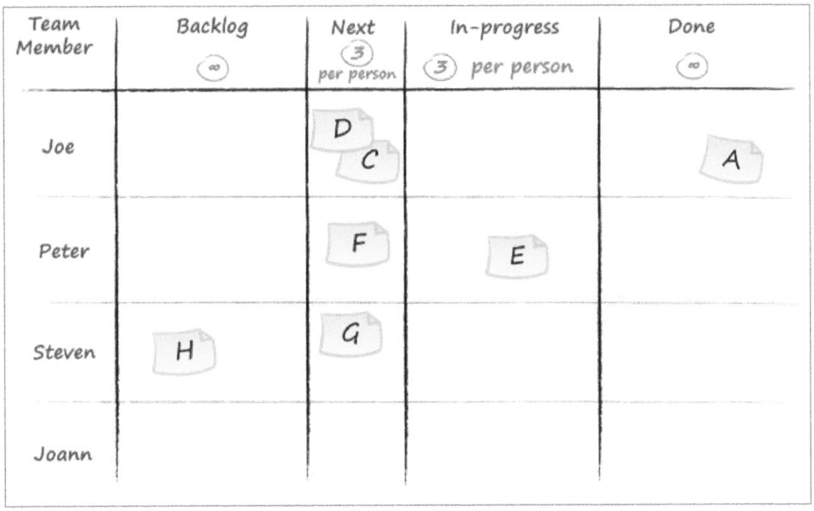

Figure 9   Aggregated personal kanban board

Description

- Use Backlog – Next – In-progress – Done columns to indicate task state.

- Use separate swim lanes for each person's work items.

- Visualize the established per-person WIP limits (see LW1.1, page 83).

Core practices

VZ1.2 Visualize the work carried out by a team by means of a team kanban board.

Description

- Use a team kanban board (Figure 10) to visualize the team's work.

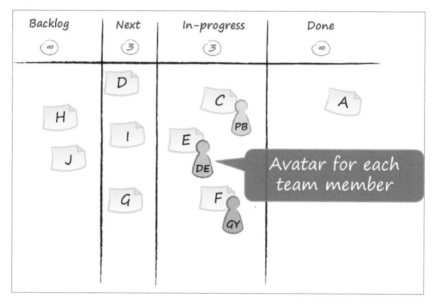

Figure 10   Team kanban board

- Use avatars to visualize current team focus (VZ1.3, below).

- Visualize WIP limits on active (In-progress) and committed (Next) work. The WIP limits are still established per person, however, the column WIP limit shows the total number of cards that can reside in the column for all team members.

VZ1.3 Use avatars to visualize each individual's workload.

Description

- For each team member, use an avatar to indicate which work items he or she is currently focused on.

- Different avatars can be used to indicate if the person is accountable for the work item or is collaborating on it.

- Each work item in-progress has an avatar of the team member accountable for it and the collaborators, if any.

VZ1.4 Visualize initial policies.

See XP1.1 (page 121) about how to define initial policies. The intent of visualizing policies is to facilitate consistency in applying them.

Description

There are different means to visualize policies, for instance:

- Write down the policies on a piece of paper and stick it next to the physical kanban board. These may also be known as "Working Norms" or "Team Norms."

- Define and visualize the policies in the electronic kanban board if its functionality allows it.

VZ1.5 Visualize teamwork by means of an emergent workflow kanban board.

Description

- Use an emergent workflow kanban board (Figure 11) to visualize work performed by the team. The board is similar to a team kanban board but has a wider In-progress column to represent work item development progress.

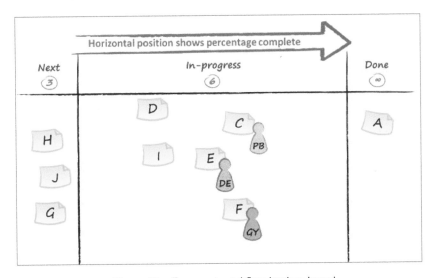

Figure 11   Emergent workflow kanban board

- Evaluate task completeness qualitatively or quantitatively using your organization's method. Position each ticket at the point in the In-progress column that represents the percentage of completion of the corresponding work item.

- As the team's understanding of the workflow gets deeper, the In-progress column can be split into columns that illustrate the main stages of the workflow.

Maturity Level 2

Transition practices

VZ2.1 Visualize teamwork by means of a delivery kanban board with per-person WIP limits.

Description

- Use a delivery kanban board (Figure 12) to visualize the principal stages of the workflow. For example:

- Pending – Specify – Development Ready – Development – Done

- Pending – Analyze – Deliver – Done

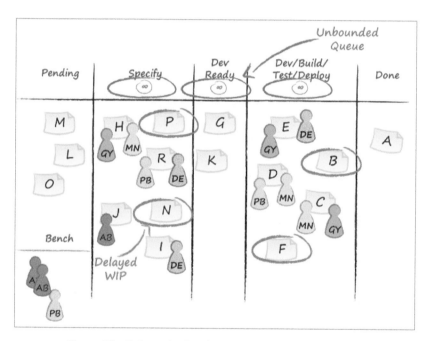

Figure 12   Delivery kanban board with per-person WIP limits

- Visualize per-person WIP limits by means of avatars, allowing a low number of avatars per individual.

In case a person works on a work item and collaborates with or assists somebody else on other work items, some variations of the avatars can be used; for example, a larger one for a work item that the person owns and a smaller one for in-collaboration work items.

VZ2.2 Visualize work types by means of card colors or board rows.

Description

- Establish a coloring scheme for visualizing work item types defined in MF2.1.

- Alternatively, use separate rows on the kanban board to visualize different work types.

- If work items are categorized by size, work items with different sizes can be represented (on physical kanban boards) by means of different-sized cards.

VZ2.3 Visualize blocked work items.

A blocking issue is something that was not anticipated that prevents continuing work on a ticket, for example, waiting for information or permission; dependence on another team, customer, or provider; temporarily moving a team member with specific knowledge to another project or service; a need to collect additional information; and so on.

Blocked issues reduce flow and cause delay of product or service delivery. To lessen these effects, it is important to see the blocked work items, understand the reasons for the blockages, and resolve them quickly.

In addition, the information collected about the blockers and its analysis (blocker clustering) is fundamental for adequately managing risks in future projects and services.

Description

- Select a symbol to indicate that a work item is blocked.

- It can be drawn manually on the tickets if a physical board is used. Electronic kanban tools provide visual means for showing that a work item is blocked. With magnetic physical boards, the color of the magnet may be changed to indicate the blocked state.

- Attach a ticket of a different color to the blocked one, as shown in Figure 13 (on the next page), explaining the reason for the blockage and additional data that would facilitate further analysis and learning—such as date of blockage, date of unblocking the ticket, main causes for the issue, who is assigned to resolve it, resolution effort, and so on. Different colors of blocker tickets may be used to signify different reasons for blocking or different sources of delay.

- Visualizing the blocked items is a first step to raising awareness of the impact of blocking issues and to focus the organization on resolving them quickly, as well as for developing the capability to do so.

- Refer to MF2.3 (page 92) for more information about managing blocking issues.

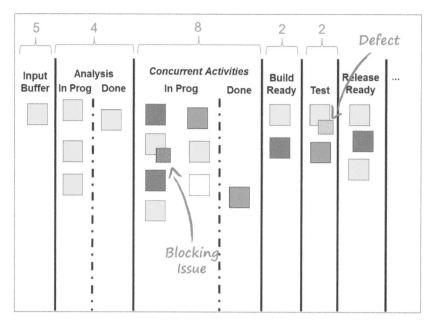

Figure 13   Kanban board showing blocked items using blocker tickets

VZ2.4 Visualize development of options by means of a discovery kanban board.

The intent of a discovery kanban board is to facilitate the development of a stream of options (ideas, incoming requests) before they covert into committed work.

Description

- The discovery kanban board could be as simple as the one illustrated in Figure 14, which shows the main steps in elaborating options.

- A ticket is used to visualize an idea/option.

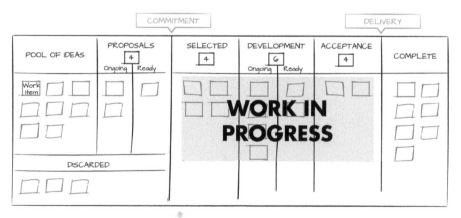

Figure 14   Initial discovery kanban board

VZ2.5 Visualize individual workload on a discovery kanban board by means of per-person WIP limits, potentially implemented using avatars.

An option is an idea or concept that is available for selection for commitment and delivery. Options must be developed by learning about them, gathering information from, for example, scientific research, market research, risk assessment, business analysis, and so on. Doing so frequently involves individuals who also work downstream, that is, those who have assignments on the delivery kanban board. Creating a smooth flow of options without affecting the delivery workflow requires proper management of an individual's availability.

Description

Extend the per-person WIP limits to include the discovery kanban board's work items as well, and visualize these limits, for example, by means of avatars.

VZ2.6 Visualize basic policies.

See XP2.2 (page 121) for guidelines about how to elaborate further policies.

Visualizing policies contributes to developing a shared understanding of the process and identifying potential improvement opportunities.

Description

Policies can be built into the design of a physical board, for example, using physical space or tokens such as magnets or sticky clips to indicate kanbans. A WIP limit for an activity can be displayed at the top of a column. A capacity allocation for a work item type or a class of service can be displayed on a row of the board. Policies that indicate "pullable," that is, a specific activity is complete, can be printed and displayed at the bottom of the column. Service level agreements may be visualized as progress bars on tickets or on a legend printed and attached to the side of the board.

Electronic kanban tools visualize policies in different manners, for example, by changing the color of a column if its WIP limit is exceeded, showing the criteria for "done" for a column at the bottom of it, using a symbol for a blocked card and impeding its movement, stating the work item size on the card, and so on.

Core practices

VZ2.7 Ticket design: Visualize concurrent or unordered activities with checkboxes.

Some In-progress columns can include several activities that can be performed in any order or in parallel. In addition, different people can work on a single ticket.

One way to manage such cases is to visualize the concurrent or unordered activities with checkboxes.

Description

- Represent different activities for a work item with checkboxes.

- When all checkboxes are checked off, the work for this ticket in this column is considered completed (Figure 15).

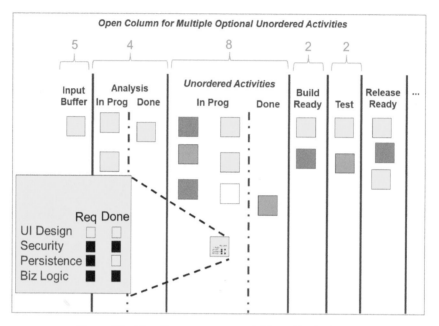

Figure 15 Visualize concurrent activities with checkboxes

VZ2.8 Ticket design: Visualize concurrent activities performed by specialist teams using partial rows.

Sometimes specialist services can and should be performed in parallel. This can be visualized by splitting one or more columns into two or more rows to visualize the flow through each specialist service.

Description

- As shown in Figure 16, create partial rows spanning one or more activity columns where specialist services should be performed in parallel. Label each row to show which service it represents

- Each ticket, when arriving at the concurrent working point, should be split by creating two or more new tickets. When sticky notes are used, the original can be stuck behind one of the new ones. When all the tickets from the split have arrived at their destination to the right-hand side of the partial rows, then they can be "merged" by discarding them and revealing the original ticket to flow to completion on the board.

Note: Kanban software tools have been unable to implement this pattern due to its impact on metrics and reporting. The workaround is to create two or more partial rows, as shown Figure 16, and two or more child tickets, where the software supports hierarchical work items, and flow the children tickets through their respective partial rows, only moving the parent ticket to the right of the split section after all of the children have arrived at the end of their partial rows. Software that doesn't support hierarchical work-item types is not suitable for use with this practice.

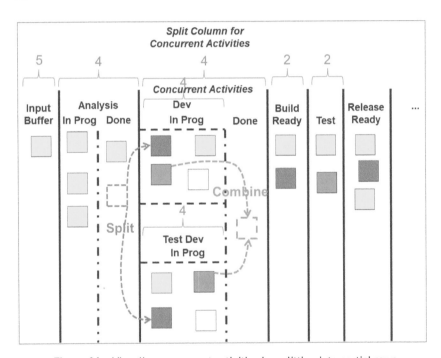

Figure 16   Visualize concurrent activities by splitting into partial rows.

VZ2.9 Board design: Visualize sequential activities where no dependency or preferred sequence exists using rows or vertical spaces.

This practice defines an alternative to VZ2.7 (page 53) for visualizing a non-linear sequence of activities.

Description

- When the work to be done within the column requires different specialist skills, split the column into different specialist areas as shown in Figure 17. Similarly, split the ticket to represent the work to be done by different specialists.

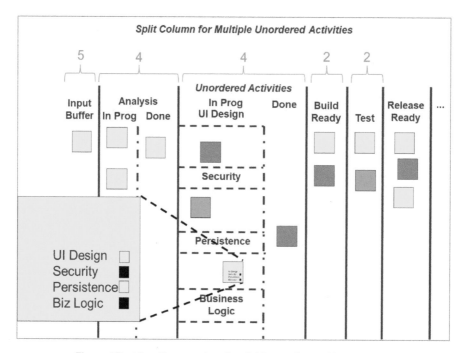

Figure 17 Visualize unordered activities performed by specialists

Required activities can be indicated using checkboxes on the ticket.

In this case, different WIP limits can be defined for the specialist areas of the column. This pattern is particularly popular if there is a belief that one specialist activity is a source of delay or a capacity-constrained resource (or bottleneck).

VZ2.10 Visualize defects and other rework types.

Awareness is the first step toward reducing defects and other rework types.

Description

- Design the rework ticket visualizing the following information:
  - ID of the work item to which the rework is associated
  - Title or brief description of the rework item
  - Date when the rework was generated

o Due date

o Severity

- Use a separate color for rework tickets to make them easily visible.

- Visualize the individuals who carry out the rework the same way as for the other work items.

- Refer to MF2.4 (page 93) for details about how to manage defects and other rework types, as well as XP2.4 (page 122) for guidelines about defining relevant policies.

VZ2.11 Use constant WIP (CONWIP) with an emergent workflow delivery kanban board to provide both workflow-level relief from overburdening and basic mechanics of a pull system with separate replenishment and delivery cadences.

A delivery kanban board, with defined commitment point and constant WIP (Figure 18), is a pull system with a basic definition of the workflow. Therefore, it allows the team to obtain a better understanding of how service delivery or product development really occurs.

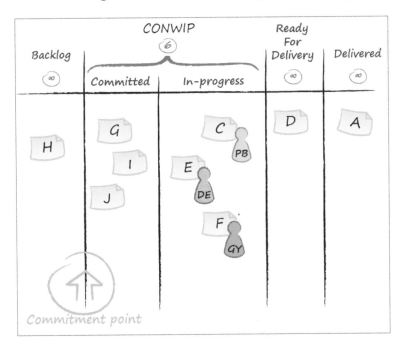

Figure 18   Delivery kanban board with defined commitment point and constant WIP

Description

- Visualize the workflow stages by means of separate columns in the In-progress area of the kanban board.

- Visualize the established CONWIP for the system (see LW2.2 on page 84 for more details about establishing constant WIP limits).

- Establish and visualize the commitment point for the kanban system. This is the point at which the team has a good understanding of the work to develop, the customer is committed to receive developed result, and the lead time starts to count.

VZ2.12 Visualize workflow by means of enhanced discovery/delivery boards.

Description

Both discovery and delivery kanban boards are modelled so as to reflect the work item process stages (see MF2.2, page 91). They are usually named for the dominant activity used to generate new information or move the work item toward completion (e.g., "test"). A defined workflow may be a superset of all states for the collection of work item types it visualizes. This takes into account that not all work items need to go through the same steps.

The Discovery part of the workflow represents the steps through which an idea evolves and converts into a committed request, for example, *Opportunity – Synthesis – Analysis*. In the opportunity stage, an idea is rather rough, overall, unclarified. In the synthesis stage, the idea becomes more coherent and clearer. During the analysis phase, the option is split into detailed work items that, once committed, are ready to be pulled into the delivery kanban system. See [13] for more details on upstream kanban.

The delivery part of the workflow visualizes the steps through which a committed work element develops into a value-adding deliverable.

VZ2.13 Visualize project progress on a portfolio kanban board.

Description

- Use a portfolio kanban board (Figure 19) to visualize an organization's projects' progress. A kanban card represents something deliverable, meaningful, and valuable to the requester, such as a single project, a minimal viable product, (MVP), or a minimum marketable feature (MMF).

- Use different colors to visualize project types, project requesters (customers), or significant project risks such as cost of delay or immovable delivery dates (such as those associated with regulatory requirements or major world events such as the Olympic Games).

- Use kanban cards of different sizes to visualize project size category; for example, small cards for small projects, medium-size tickets for medium-size projects, and large tickets for large projects. Slightly deeper maturity implementations will have a defined, explicit policy designating project size—for example, large involves more than fifty people or $5 million in budget.

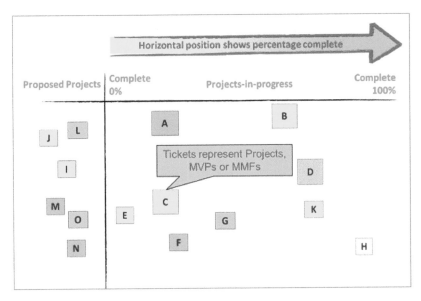

Figure 19   Portfolio kanban board

- Use the horizontal axis of the In-progress column to represent project progress, and position ongoing project tickets so as to visualize their % Complete.

- Include the not-yet-started projects in the Proposed Projects column.

Maturity Level 3

Transition practices

VZ3.1 Visualize "ready to commit" status, also known as "ready to pull."

Description

Work items that are ready to pull into the kanban system and/or ready to be committed for work and future delivery are visualized using a physical space or position on the board, such as a column indicating the status of tickets placed within it.

VZ3.2 Visualize "ready to pull criteria," also known as "definition of ready," or "entry criteria."

Description

Policies required to enter the "ready to commit" or "ready to pull" state are explicitly defined and visualized.

VZ3.3 Visualize workflow and teamwork items by means of an aggregated teams kanban board.

Use an aggregated teams kanban board to visualize on a single board the work carried out by different teams on adjacent steps in a workflow, for example, customer specifications, development, or development-testing (Figure 20).

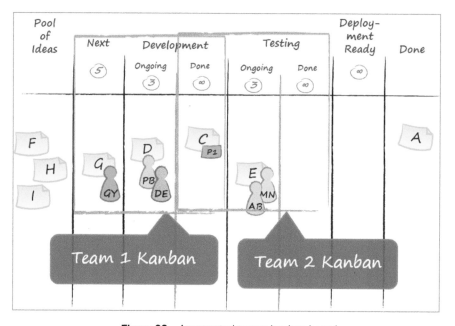

Figure 20   Aggregated teams kanban board

Description

- Use team kanban boards to visualize the work of each team.

- Visualize the WIP limits for the team kanban systems.

- Use the queue of delivered work from the first-step team as an input queue for the second-step team. This queue can remain unbounded.

- Refer to LW1.2 and LW2.1 (both on page 84) for more details on establishing team and activity-based WIP limits.

VZ3.4 Visualize project work items on a two-tiered project kanban board.

Description

- Use a two-tiered portfolio kanban board to visualize the state of each project (Figure 21).

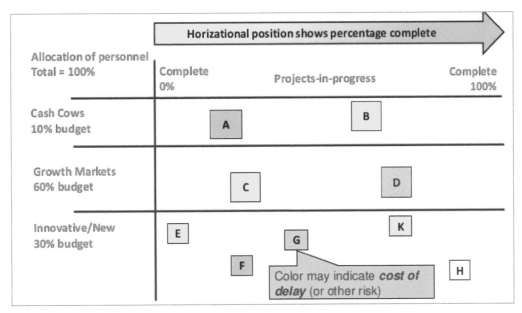

Figure 21 Two-tiered project kanban board

- Similarly to the simple portfolio kanban board, use tickets to represent individual projects or key project results.

- Use separate swim lanes to indicate different project types.

- Position the tickets in the Projects-in-progress column as to visualize their % Complete.

VZ3.5 Visualize parent–child and peer–peer dependencies.

Parent–child dependencies emerge when a work item is broken down to the elements that comprise it. A parent work item is considered done only when all its child work items are successfully completed and integrated. Child work items can reside on different boards than their parent card.

Peer-to-peer relationships define dependencies between work items at the same level. Typically, these are work items that have to be finished in a particular sequence, or items that must be delivered together in order to enable something of customer value; a metaphorical example is that you cannot go skiing without both the skis and the boots—there is a mutual dependency between the boots and the skis in the context of a day on the mountain skiing, while the production and delivery of skis can happen entirely independently from the boots.

Description

- Define a manner of visualizing each type of dependency: parent–child or peer–peer. It could be a symbol, for example, an arrow whose direction indicates which work item is a child or successor, respectively; the type of line can indicate the type of relationship (parent–child or peer–peer).

- Annotate on the card references to the dependent work items:

  o Those that depend on it (parent work item) and such that it depends on (child work items);

  o Those that precede (predecessors) or have to be implemented after it (successors).

Electronic boards use different means or tags to visualize dependencies of parent–child and peer–peer types between work items.

VZ3.6 Use a parking lot to visualize work requests dependent on another service or system currently waiting or blocked.

Dependencies between work items typically occur when different individuals or teams are involved in doing the job. Not managing dependencies correctly increases risks for delays or quality issues. Therefore, it is important to visualize them consistently.

When there are dependencies on external groups (other teams, customer, suppliers), it is appropriate to use a parking lot to visualize them.

Description

- Use tickets with pre-defined colors to indicate work items that depend on an external group.

- Designate a special area of the kanban board, a parking lot, for sticking the tickets that represent this work (see Figure 22).

- Stick the card representing the work item to be implemented by an external group in the parking lot.

- There are variants of this pattern that may involve spawning a new ticket with peer–peer dependency on the original. The new peer is placed in the parking lot and a visual indicator such as a smaller ticket of similar color is placed on the ticket that spawned the external request. See VZ2.3 (page 51), visualizing blockers.

- Deeper maturity organizations will create explicit policy around dependencies including WIP limits for the dependent items parking lot and service level agreements or expectations (SLAs or SLEs) for the processing time of dependent items, as well as procedures for escalation when dependent items are taking too long and causing delay (see VZ4.6 and VZ4.7).

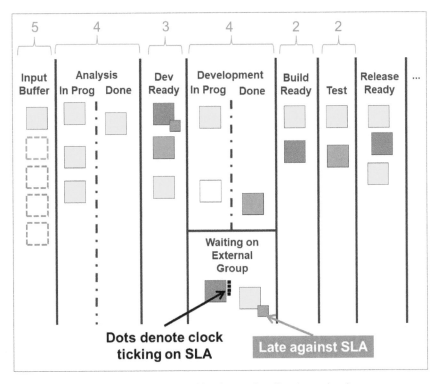

Figure 22   Using parking lot to visualize dependencies

Figure 20 illustrates tracking time blocked items using tally marks on the right-hand side of a ticket in the parking lot and then escalating with a pink blocker ticket if the dependent service fails to meet its SLA.

Core practices

VZ3.7 Visualize upstream options by means of an upstream/discovery kanban board.

The process of elaborating ideas to be developed and delivered to customers and end users is in itself a triage process. Each idea goes through several steps of refinement before finally being selected for development or discarded.

The purpose of the upstream, or "discovery," kanban board is to properly manage customers' ideas, make clear what their status is, and show which ideas are closer to validation and ready or available to be committed and pulled into the delivery stream. Instead of handling a single unordered list of customer requests, the discovery kanban board allows the team to focus their efforts on elaborating options, concentrating first on those that can be replenished to the delivery team while elaborating further other alternatives.

Description

- Use an upstream kanban board to visualize the state of possible options (Figure 23).

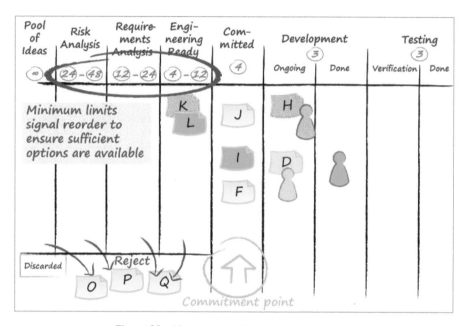

Figure 23 Upstream, or discovery, kanban board

The commitment point separates the discovery from the delivery kanban board. Only requests that the customer is sure they want delivered have to pass the border between the two systems.

It is common for a discovery board to be separate from a delivery board. Often discovery and delivery are performed by separate organizations, and in many larger enterprises these functions do not sit together. Hence, it is more natural to have two boards rather than just one, as illustrated in Figure 23.

VZ3.8 Visualize discarded options using a bin on an upstream/discovery kanban board.

It is useful to show discarded options for a period of time immediately after discarding. This allows for reflection on whether alternatives were better choices and whether an option has been appropriately discarded.

Description

Create a space on an upstream/discovery kanban board or a bin to the left of the commitment point on a delivery kanban board, and actively display recently discarded tickets

(Figure 24). Define policy to determine how long a ticket should be displayed before it is removed, for example, one month.

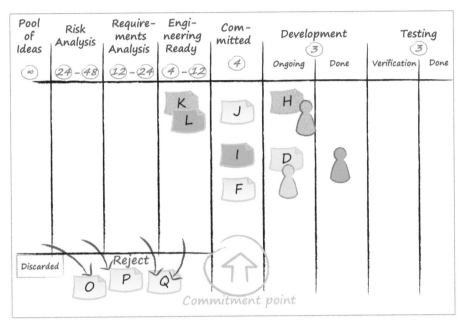

Figure 24   Discarded options bin

VZ3.9 Visualize replenishment signals.

Kanban tokens may be used to visualize replenishment of a kanban system. Alternatively, a virtual kanban mechanism can be used to indicate pull (VZ3.10).

Description

- Use movable tokens such as magnets on a magnetic white board to represent replenishment signals (see Figure 25).
- The number of magnets in circulation represents the WIP limit.
- The color of a magnet indicates whether it is pullable or not.

VZ3.10 Visualize pull signals.

Description

The virtual kanban board in Figure 25 shows a kanban board on which having fewer work item cards in a column than the WIP limit displayed on the top of it indicates pull. The signals are virtual, hence the board is known as virtual kanban board.

VZ3.11 Visualize pull criteria (also known as "pull policies," "definition of done," or "exit criteria").

See XP3.5 (page 125) for more details about how to define pull criteria.

Description

There are different means to visualize pull criteria:

- Stick the list of pull criteria next to a physical kanban board or at the place where daily and Delivery Planning Meetings take place.

- Stick the list of "done" criteria above each column of the kanban board.

- Visualize the pull criteria using relevant functionality of your electronic kanban tool.

VZ3.12 Visualize available capacity.

Description

There are different means to visualize the available capacity:

- Physical slots

- Movable tokens

- Virtual kanban

A free slot, magnet, or sticky clip in a column is a signal for pulling work from the column that is immediately before it. Having fewer cards in a column than the virtual kanban number also indicates that a work item can be pulled from the column before.

The physical slot kanban board is designed to serve teams that tend to deviate from established WIP limits. Therefore, it explicitly shows the places from where work items can be pulled.

On the movable tokens kanban board, the number of magnets represents the WIP limits. The color of the magnets shows the status of the work item: in-progress, done, blocked. This board provides more flexibility to the team as magnets can be moved, added, or removed dynamically. However, it also requires more discipline in handling the number of tokens so as to ensure consistent outcome of the process.

VZ3.13 Visualize work item aging.

Card aging shows the amount of time (e.g., days, hours) a work item has been in the delivery kanban system since commitment. For a discovery board, this is the amount of time since the idea was first introduced.

Work item aging is an indicator of potential problems because the longer a work item is in progress, the higher the risk of not delivering on time (or not meeting SLAs), suffering change requests, or a decision to abort due to not responding to the customer's evolved expectations. It is well understood in risk management that the longer something is delayed, the greater the possibility of further delay being introduced, that is, there is an increasing hazard rate associated with delay.

Description

These are some alternatives to visualize aging:

- Use a progress bar on the ticket.

- Use tally marks on a designated section of the ticket (one mark per day).

- Visualize the time (e.g., in days or hours) since pulling the work item in the system.

- Some software kanban solutions visualize aging by means of gradually dulling the color of the ticket to create a withering effect.

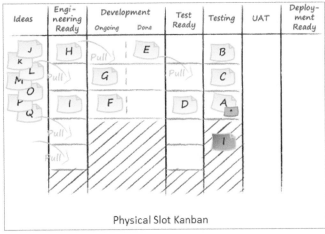

Physical Slot Kanban

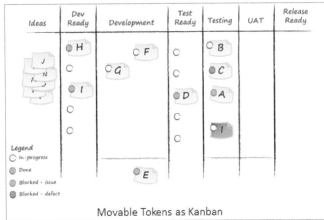

Movable Tokens as Kanban

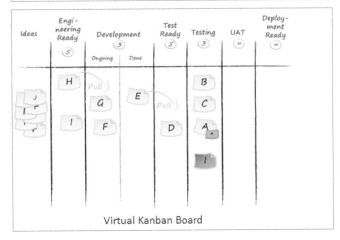

Virtual Kanban Board

Figure 25 Visualizing available capacity

VZ3.14 Visualize target date or SLA.

Refer to XP3.7 (page 126) about defining classes of service.

Establishing a target lead time for a class of service eliminates the need to estimate, negotiate, and commit to each work item individually.

Description

Consider the following two alternatives for visualizing target date (Figure 26):

- Indicate on the ticket the threshold date as per the SLA as well as the due date.

- Mark the threshold date on a progress bar (a row of cells, one for each day of the agreed time) such that elapsed time and remaining time until the threshold are clearly visible.

Figure 26   Ticket showing due date, progress bar, and SLA lead-time target

VZ3.15 Visualize failure demand versus value demand.

Failure demand represents work item demand generated as a consequence of previous poor-quality deliverables. Failure demand is avoidable if initial quality is better matched to customer expectations. Failure demand includes defect fix requests, rework due to usability problems, rework due to poor design or misunderstanding of customer needs, and features requested by the users because other functionality did not work (workarounds).

Description

- Use a color of ticket or a ticket decorator to indicate which work items are failure demand. It may be appropriate to have explicit work item types for failure demand and hence, all items of that type are known to be failure demand, for example, "usability fix."

- Use graphics (e.g., pie charts, bar charts, Pareto diagrams) to visualize the amount of failure demand as well as the causes for them.

- Analyze the causes for the failure demand.

- Plot on graphs the quantitative summary of the analysis.

Failure demand may be shared at the Service Delivery Review, Risk Review, and/or Operations Review in order to drive corrective improvement actions intended to reduce it.

VZ3.16 Visualize aborted work.

Aborted work is work for which all of the following facts are true:

- It was started, committed, and a customer indicated they wished to take delivery.
- The delivery organization indicated that they were ready and committed to doing the work and delivering the finished work product.
- For some reason, the work was aborted before completion.

Such work wastes capacity within the system and diminishes the delivery capability. It is desirable to avoid starting work that will not make it to completion.

Description

- Use a trash can to collect all the tickets representing work items that have been aborted (Figure 27).
- Use graphs (e.g., pie charts, bar charts, Pareto diagrams) or spreadsheets to visualize the amount of aborted demand and the reason the work was aborted.
- Analyze the causes for aborted demand.
- Plot on graphs the quantitative summary of the analysis.

Aborted demand should be reported at the Replenishment Meeting and, optionally, at Service Delivery Review, Risk Review, and/or Operations Review.

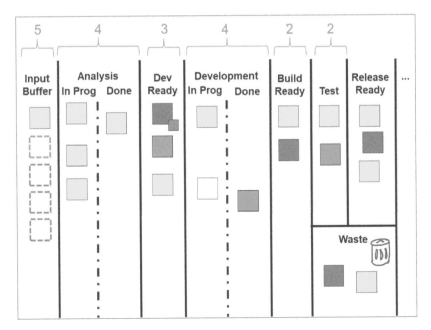

Figure 27   Waste bin for aborted work items

VZ3.17 Visualize class of service using ticket colors, board rows, or ticket decorators.

A class of service is a set of policies that describe how something should be treated. Policy is usually aligned to risks associated with an item, or perhaps the value or price paid to process the item. Multiple classes of service are commonly used to extract additional economic performance from a system, or align delivery to differing customer expectations.

Low maturity organizations, ML2 and below, will typically treat all work homogeneously, or have no explicit policy on class of service, hence, visualizing them all homogeneously, with the possible exception of an "expedite" class of service. Organizations that rely on individual or managerial heroics often need a process to facilitate the heroic effort—an explicit definition of an expedite class of service facilitates this.

A more sophisticated understanding of risk, customer expectations, and the possibilities enabled through multiple classes of service emerges in the transition to ML3. Organizations transitioning to ML3 typically focus classes of service on policy providing guidance on priority of pull. This aligns directly to the urgency of an item. Urgency may be understood only in a qualitative manner.

At ML3, it is typical to have an explicit understanding of customer expectations (or fitness criteria for service delivery) and align classes of service to these expectations.

In deeper maturity organizations, at ML4 and beyond, classes of service are aligned to sets of business risks and used to optimize economic performance as well as ensure customer satisfaction.

Assuming there is more than one way that work items are treated, then it is useful to visualize the difference in anticipated treatment.

Description

Use a defined color scheme for tickets. Typically, greater risks or higher levels of service are given warmer, or hot, colors such as red, orange or white. Lower risks or less urgent items are given colder colors such as pale blue or green. It is conventional to use pale yellow (or vanilla) for the default or "standard" class of service. This convention emerged due to the standard pale yellow sticky notes so commonly used in kanban board implementations.

Organizations often create standard work policies for use of color in kanban boards. This enables more senior managers and external stakeholders to correctly interpret the meaning of colors across all boards within the same product or business unit.

Alternatively, use a horizontal lane on a board for each class of service, labeling the lane with the name of the class of service. It is common to use this technique for expedite requests and to have such a lane labeled with a nickname or common-language term for expedite such as "Express Lane" or "Express Service."

VZ3.18 Use Earned Value portfolio kanban board to visualize project progress and schedule or budget risk.

Managing large projects requires keeping control on additional aspects such as percentage of scope complete, usage of budget, and scheduled time. In addition to coordinating several projects, shared resources, and dependencies, portfolio project management takes care of maximizing the outcome from the set of projects as a whole. The Earned Value portfolio kanban board visualizes the key information necessary for this.

Description

Use an advanced version of portfolio kanban board that visualizes the following aspects of the projects (Figure 28):

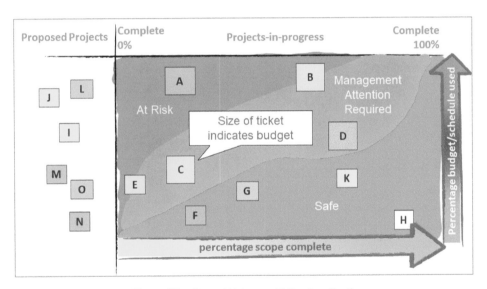

Figure 28 Earned Value portfolio visualization

- Horizontal axis: percentage of scope complete

- Vertical axis: budget and schedule usage

- Size of the ticket: classification of the economic size of the project (based on its budget)

- Position the ongoing projects in the In-progress area on the positions that reflect their status (% Complete).

- Stick the tickets for the projects not yet started in the Proposed Projects column.

- Use the principles of a fever chart to indicate which projects need management attention because there is a risk of not meeting their objectives within the established time and budget parameters. More precisely, projects that go well, developing the scope within time and budget, appear in the green zone on the board. Projects that do not progress as expected, but the deviation is still acceptable or manageable, appear in the amber zone on the board. Projects with significant risks of not meeting their objectives are visualized in the red board zone.

Maturity Level 4

Transition practices

VZ4.1 Visualize local cycle time.

Local cycle time is the time a work item spends in a specific activity or a defined sequence of activities. For example, local cycle time for test is the time a work item spends in the Testing column. Development cycle time is the time a work item spends in Development, before being pulled into Testing, and Development could comprise Requirement Analysis, Design, Implementation, and Unit Testing.

Knowing local cycle times is important for understanding the entire workflow and being able to identify the slowest parts of it (the bottlenecks) and the flow impediments.

We may also wish to study waiting time by measuring time in Test separately from time waiting in Ready for Test. This data contributes to calculating flow efficiency and also indicates which states impact flow efficiency the most, and hence, provide insight on where to focus improvement initiatives.

Description

Alternative approaches can be used for visualizing local cycle time:

- Use dots next to a kanban card to indicate the number of days it spends in a state (column) (Figure 29). The total number of days in the column is then recorded in a cell on the ticket at the point when the ticket is moved.

- Indicate *Date in* and *Date out* for the column in which local cycle time is being monitored.

The same ways for visualizing local cycle time can be used to visualize the time a work item is blocked, for example, waiting on an external group or customer.

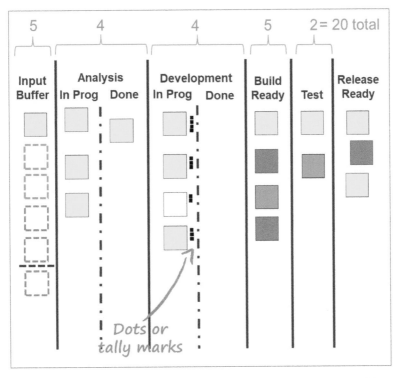

Figure 29   Visualizing local cycle time beside a ticket using dots or tallies

VZ4.2 Use ticket decorators to indicate risk.

Risk is a multi-dimensional contextual problem. Proper risk visualization facilitates understanding the risk itself and how it could affect the outcome of the service, project, or business. Risk visualization facilitates democratization of risk management, enabling workers to make good quality risk reduction or mitigation decisions. Risk visualization is a means to greater empowerment and higher levels of trust.

Designated decorators on the kanban cards can indicate to team members which specific risks are present with an item. This will inform what actions are appropriate.

Some software kanban boards are capable of adding decorators to tickets and, in some cases, displaying entire risk profiles as Kiviat charts[3] on the ticket.

Description

These are different possible means to visualize risks associated with a work item (Figure 30):

---

3. Further explanation of risk profiling and the use of Kiviat charts for visualizing risk will be provided in the KMMX for Enterprise Services Planning (ESP).

- Use card colors to indicate risks associated with cost of delay (CoD), typically caused by schedule, budget, or scope change; for example, use white for expedite, orange for fixed date, yellow for standard, and purple for intangible work items. Refer to XP3.8 (page 127) for defining classes of service. An alternative manner to visualize CoD associated risks is to designate a row on the kanban board for each class of service.

- Indicate the due date and actual end date for the work item to signal a delay risk.

- Use a row of cells, one for each day of the agreed time. Marking the age of the ticket on this row clearly shows the risk of not meeting the SLA.

- Use checkboxes to visualize technical or skill set risks related to the work item.

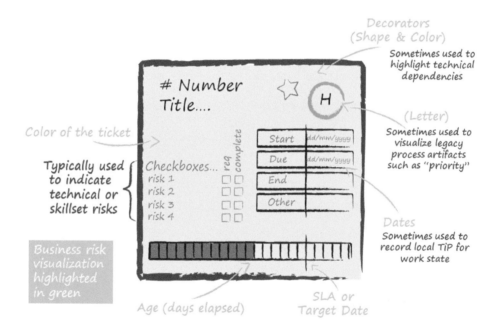

Figure 30   Using decorators to indicate risks

VZ4.3 Visualize risk classes with different swim lanes.

Kanban boards have three very obvious dimensions available for communicating important information. The horizontal position tends to be used to communicate the sequence of workflow stages and item's state of completion within that workflow. The vertical position and the ticket color are available to communicate the two most important risks. Less significant risks must be deferred to ticket decorators or left not visualized altogether.

Description

Decide the two most important risk dimensions under management. Pick one of these two to be displayed using vertical position on the board. For each risk category in the taxonomy for the dimension, draw and label a lane on the board.

All work items carrying that specific risk category will be placed on the appropriate lane (Figure 31).

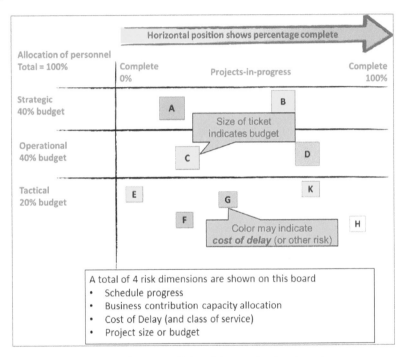

Figure 31   Visualizing risks on a kanban board

VZ4.4 Visualize split-and-merge workflows.

Split-and-merge workflows occur when two or more activities or chains of activities need to happen in parallel. This pattern is most relevant when the parallel work is done by different sets of workers or is perceived as different or separate services. Sometimes, one or more of the parallel workflows are provided by external service providers. The parallel work is later merged into a single work product that continues to flow downstream for delivery. Conceptually, this is done on physical boards by "splitting" the ticket and then "merging" it back to a single ticket later. The arrival of the completed sub-elements must be coordinated so that the parallel work can be merged back into a single work item and work product. This is usually achieved with a holding buffer labeled "done" displayed as a single vertical column, spanning the two or more rows for the parallel workflows.

Description

For example, design and development may happen in parallel to test plan design and automated test development. For those columns on the board, create two rows, one for deliverable design and development and the other for the test plan design and development. When a ticket is pulled into design and development, create a second ticket and place it in the other row, using the same index number, so that its peer or sibling can be identified and the pair remerged into one after the activities are complete.

When sticky notes are used, the merge can be achieved by placing the second ticket underneath or behind the first ticket at the point of merging.

Software kanban boards do not support this split-and-merge concept. Instead, the implementation is done by creating two child tickets and using a two-tiered board solution.

The physical board split-and-merge uses rows on the board to designate the split and the merge and the different workflows. The software solution delegates the split to the ticket types. There is no concept of merge—the child tickets simply complete and the parent ticket continues to flow across the board. With software, it may make sense to use different colors to show the different types of children tickets, for example, the mainline deliverable, design and development, from the second line, test plan design and automated test development. With the physical board, different workers move tickets on different lanes; with the software, different workers move different colors (types) of tickets within the same lane (Figure 32).

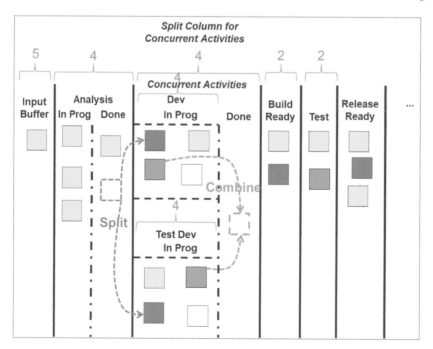

Figure 32   Visualizing split-and-merge workflow

Core practices

VZ4.5 Visualize WIP limits on a dependencies parking lot.

A WIP limit on a parking lot has the potential to stop flow altogether on a service delivery board. It is therefore a behavior of a deeper maturity organization that is prepared to cope with the stress caused by unpredictable delivery from dependent services or has already resolved the predictability issue so that problems do not occur.

Description

The WIP limit for the parking lot can be depicted by a number of physical cells on the board, one for each "parking space," that is, one per work item, or by the use of movable tokens such as magnets, one per blocked worked item, or by using a virtual kanban by writing the maximum number of permitted blocked tickets into the parking lot space on the board (Figure 33).

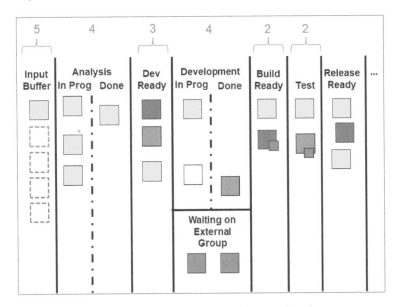

Figure 33   Visualizing blocked item parking lot

VZ4.6 Visualize waiting time in a dependencies parking lot.

It is useful to record how long an item has been blocked. This data can help to drive improvements at the Operations Review meeting and at the system of kanban systems level of scale. Visualizing waiting can also prove sufficient to motivate external groups to deliver in a timely manner.

Description

Use dots or tally marks beside a waiting ticket to denote each day of waiting (Figure 34).

When a dependent item arrives back, record the time waiting on the original ticket or the blocker ticket, if appropriate.

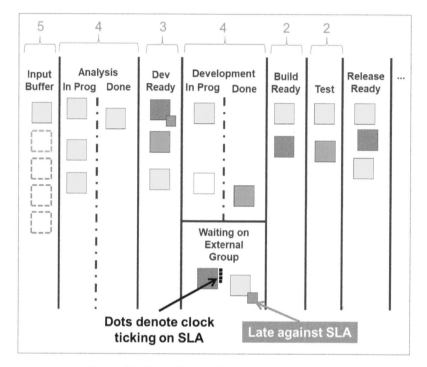

Figure 34   Recording waiting time for dependencies

VZ4.7 Visualize SLA exceeded in dependencies parking lot.

If an SLA or SLE exists with a dependent service, or kanban system, then it is useful to visualize when that SLA/SLE has been exceeded. This data can help to drive improvements at the Operations Review meeting and at the system of kanban systems level of scale. Visualizing late against an SLA can also prove sufficient to motivate an external group to accelerate.

Description

Use a small blocker ticket in a bright color to indicate a dependent request has taken longer than expected or is acceptable. When a dependent item arrives back, record the time waiting and the fact that the SLA/SLE was exceeded on the original ticket or the blocker ticket, if appropriate (Figure 35).

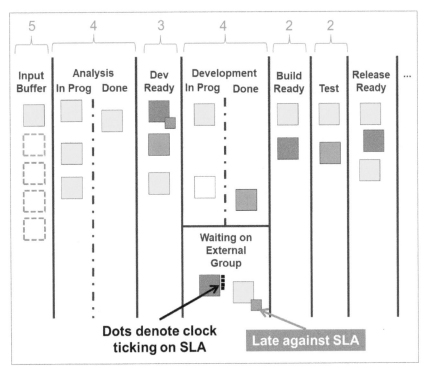

Figure 35 Visualizing exceeded SLA on a dependency

Maturity Level 5

Core practices

VZ5.1 Visualize fixed teams and floating workers (shared resources) across aggregated services.

A flexible labor pool helps to smooth flow and provides agility in response to ebb and flow of demand for work of given types or risks.

A mixture of fixed teams and flexible floating workers who have generalist, or "t-shaped," skill sets is a good solution for optimizing customer satisfaction and business agility.

Description

As shown in Figure 36, define a board with rows for specific work item types or specific categories of risk. Allocate specific teams to each work type and row on the board. Provide a column or space to write the names of each team member against the appropriate row. Indicate whether there is a hierarchy in the team or a member explicitly playing the service delivery manager (SDM) role.

For all other floating or flexible workers in the larger team or department, provide them with one or more avatars accordingly. Their avatars can be placed on any row on the board to indicate the tickets on which they are working or collaborating with fixed team members (see Figure 36).

Assignments for floating workers can be discussed at the Kanban Meeting or specifically on an on-demand or ad hoc basis with team leads or service delivery managers.

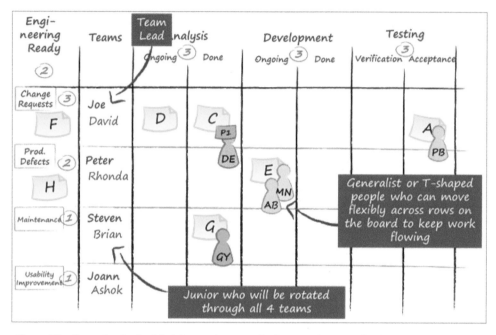

Figure 36   Example of a flexible labor pool pattern for improved system liquidity and smoother flow

6 | Limit Work-in-Progress

Goals

- To relieve individuals, functions, and service delivery systems of overburdening
- To discourage excessive and damaging multitasking
- To encourage deferred commitment
- To establish a pull system on part or all of the workflow
- To catalyze the development of triage capability

Benefits

- Allows individuals and teams to focus on work valued by the customer
- Makes the work flow through the kanban system
- Mitigates the effects of unevenness in arrival rate and flow of work
- Makes bottlenecks visible
- Makes visible delays due to non-instant availability of shared resources
- Amplifies the impact of blocking issues and encourages their early and swift resolution
- Improves value delivery rate, delivery times, and quality
- Improves predictability

- Stimulates conversations about problems in the process

- Fosters collaboration, causing people to work together on work items in order to finish them and get free capacity for the kanban system

- Facilitates achieving balance within and between kanban systems

- Facilitates process understanding

- Helps with reduction or elimination of three core types of waste: *muri* (overburdening), resulting in poor quality and rework; *mura* (unevenness), resulting in long and unpredictable lead times, encouraging early starts and more WIP, or incurring unanticipated (opportunity) cost of delay; and *muda* (non-value-adding activities), resulting in additional costs and potential delays

Specific Practices Summary

Maturity Level		Limit Work-in-Progress (LW) Practice
ML0	Core	**LW0.1** Establish personal WIP limits.
ML1	Transition	**LW1.1** Establish per-person WIP limits.
	Core	**LW1.2** Establish team WIP limits.
ML2	Transition	**LW2.1** Establish activity based WIP limits.
	Core	**LW2.2** Establish CONWIP limits on emergent workflow.
ML3	Transition	
	Core	**LW3.1** Use an order point (min limit) for upstream replenishment. **LW3.2** Use a max limit to define capacity. **LW3.3** Bracket WIP limits for different states.
ML4	Transition	
	Core	**LW4.1** Limit WIP on dependency parking lot.

Specific Practice Descriptions

Maturity Level 0

Core practices

LW0.1 Establish personal WIP limits.

Limiting work-in-progress (WIP) restricts the number of started-and-not-finished work items. This reduces multitasking and hence the lead time for delivering work. The lower the WIP limit, the less multitasking, the shorter the time for delivering results.

Description

Establish the number of work items that can reside in the In-progress and Next columns (Figure 8 on page 46).

Determine the WIP limit, empirically observing how many tickets are completed between two subsequent replenishments of the Next column.

Initially, the "personal tasks" list is unlimited and usually long. A rule of thumb is to start limiting the WIP gradually, until reaching two or three tasks in progress.

There is research in psychology suggesting two or three things in-progress simultaneously is optimal, producing the best outcome for efficiency (personal loading), quality, lead time, and completion rate. Regularly completing work provides a sense of achievement and motivation to continue. Small things achieved frequently have a greater positive impact than a large thing or batch of things completed infrequently.

Maturity Level 1

Transition practices

LW1.1 Establish per-person WIP limits.

Description

- Establish empirically the number of work items that can be In-progress within the lane for a person on the kanban board. Try to codify the size of an individual work item against a single unit of WIP, for example, no ticket should involve more than two days of work for an individual working without interruption.

- For teams that are used to managing work in terms of working hours, an appropriate

> **Coaching Tip:** Take into consideration the size of the work items. Excessively large work items move too slowly through the system. When tickets don't show visible, regular progress across the board, they are hard to manage: is the ticket blocked, or is the work too large, too complex, or overly elaborate? People also become disengaged with kanban boards when there is no animation to it. If tickets aren't moving then there is no new information and hence, why hold a Kanban Meeting? Use this tension to motivate new analysis behavior to break work down to smaller chunks.

per-person WIP limit would be approximately the number of work items that can be delivered in a couple of days.

LW1.2 Establish team WIP limits.

Unlike per-person WIP limits, establishing team WIP limits fosters collaboration, speeds up delivery, increases workflow efficiency, and facilitates knowledge sharing. In addition, team WIP limits build the culture of "delivering customer value together." Team members start swarming around work items that require joint work trying to understand and resolve them together. A team WIP limit is the first step to viewing a group of individuals who collaborate together as a system. A team WIP limit aims to avoid overburdening the team as a system rather than any one individual.

Description

- Empirically establish the WIP limit for the entire team.

- Observe what causes breaking the established team WIP limit. Make sure that team members do not start new work items or stay idle instead of swarming on larger tasks or tasks with associated issues.

Tip: Start with the sum of work items per person for the entire team and reduce them gradually. Iterate this until reaching a state at which everyone has a ticket to work on and nobody is multitasking.

Maturity Level 2

Transition practices

LW2.1 Establish activity-based WIP limits.

Description

- Establish the number of work items that can reside in a column that represents a particular activity. All work items carried out by the entire team count in this WIP limit, both not blocked and blocked.

- When a WIP limit for a column is established and there are several lanes within it (one per person), the WIP limit is the total number of work items in all the lanes.

Core practices

LW2.2 Establish constant WIP (CONWIP) limits on emergent workflow.

The CONWIP defines the number of work items in the Committed and In-progress columns all together, no matter what their type and size are. This is a manner to create a pull system in which a work item enters only when another one is completed and has exited the system. A CONWIP pull system keeps less tight control on the cards in each state of the workflow (column) and is easier to implement, but we consider it a Proto-Kanban system.

Description

Determine the CONWIP by taking into account the capacity of the people working on the board. If CONWIP is higher than the actual capacity of the team, some persons will do multitasking. If the CONWIP is lower than actual team capacity, someone will be idle.

Maturity Level 3

Core practices

LW3.1 Use an order point (min limit) for upstream replenishment.

Description

The min limit for the upstream kanban board ensures a steady flow of ideas and options. Downstream functions should never starve for lack of input.

Hitting the min limit point is a signal for replenishment by demanding the upstream system produce more.

See LW3.2 about using max limit for an upstream kanban board.

LW3.2 Use a max limit to define capacity.

Each ticket on an upstream kanban board represents an option, a potential request for the downstream team.

Description

The max limit serves to protect the upstream function from overburdening. Workers developing options—performing experiments, designs, or otherwise discovering new information—will still suffer from overburdening and undue multitasking if too many tasks are in-progress together. A max limit prevents such overburdening from becoming troublesome.

See LW3.1 about establishing a min limit for an upstream kanban board.

LW3.3 Bracket WIP limits for different states.

It is common to use a Done sub-column to visualize that a completed work item is ready to be pulled to the next activity. For example, as shown on Figure 37, when testing a work item is finished, the kanban card that represents it is moved to the Done sub-column of the Test column, which is a queue.

It is a common mistake to view the activity and its Done as two separate states that require separate WIP limits, when in fact, the Done state merely signals that an item is "pullable."

A correct solution is to visualize the WIP limit across both states, using curled brackets and clearly showing two sub-columns, In-Progress and Done, from a single activity.

The technique can be extended across multiple activity columns. This is commonly done when work is "flowed" through several activities by generalist workers who do not concede ownership of a ticket when a single activity is completed. As there is no "pull" between activities when work is flowed by a generalist or craft worker, there is no need for separate WIP limits.

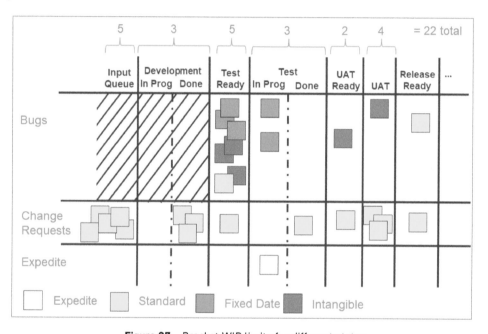

Figure 37   Bracket WIP limits for different states

The technique of bracketing WIP limits across states, or across activities and sub-columns, is used to indicate handoffs between workers and determine where "pull" is necessary. It is desirable to avoid unbounded queues or buffers, as this breaks the integrity of the pull system and has consequences for long and less predictable lead time.

Description

- Empirically determine the WIP limit for the two states.
  The overall idea is that the WIP limit should protect the workers from overburdening while providing enough slack to absorb variability in local cycle times for adjacent activities, enabling a reasonable balance between loading (or worker efficiency) and flow efficiency (or the time a ticket spends waiting between activities).

- Bracket WIP limit across In-progress and Done sub-columns for a given activity.

Note: When an alternative method is used to visually signal "pullable" when an activity is completed, this technique of bracketing WIP limits is obviated. For example, some software tools signal "pullable" by bordering the ticket in bright green. In such designs there are no In-progress and Done sub-columns.

Maturity Level 4

Core practices

LW4.1 Limit WIP on a dependency parking lot.

Description

A dependency parking lot, as shown in Figure 38, buffers work between one kanban system and another. If the dependent system exhibits stability and predictable lead times, then it is possible to limit WIP in the dependency buffer without causing too much stress. Even if the dependent system doesn't exhibit stability and predictability, a WIP can still be set on the buffer. The WIP limit will act as a stressor, potentially causing upstream stalling within the kanban system. This stress can be discussed at a Service Delivery Review (see FL3.4, page 138) and escalated at an Operations Review (see FL4.3, page 142).

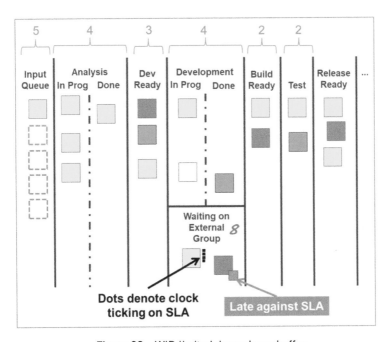

Figure 38 WIP-limited dependency buffer

Buffer sizing, or the value for the WIP limit, can be estimated using Little's Law. If we know the average arrival rate in the calling kanban system, and the average lead time from the called (dependent) system, then we can calculate the average WIP. The WIP limit should be set slightly higher than the average WIP.

WIP will tend to vary over time and exhibit a Gaussian distribution. Assuming the dependency parking lot buffer was previously unbounded, a study of historical data will suggest an upper limit, and the new WIP limit should be set somewhere between the upper limit and the mean calculated using Little's Law.

The WIP limit can be empirically adjusted and should be a topic of discussion at Service Delivery Reviews until a stable value has been realized.

7 | Manage Flow

Goal

To achieve fast, smooth, and predictable creation and delivery of customer value, minimizing risk and cost of delay.

Benefits

- Affords a deep understanding of the types of demand and how they are processed to deliver customer value
- Identifies impediments in the workflow and defines how to eliminate them
- Improves delivery predictability
- Improves workflow efficiency
- Establishes classes of service
- Allows development of a quantitative understanding of the entire process and how to use it to manage better the capacity of the kanban systems, the workflow, and customer satisfaction
- Improves forecasting
- Improves risk management
- Improves optionality by enabling ever-later deferral of commitment

Specific Practices Summary

Maturity Level		Manage Flow (MF) Practice
ML0	Core	**MF0.1** Define work types based on nature of tasks.
ML1	Transition	
	Core	
ML2	Transition	**MF2.1** Define work types based on customer requests.
	Core	**MF2.2** Map upstream and downstream flow. **MF2.3** Manage blocking issues. **MF2.4** Manage defects and other rework types.
ML3	Transition	**MF3.1** Organize around the knowledge discovery process. **MF3.2** Defer commitment (decide at the "last responsible moment.") **MF3.3** Use cumulative flow diagram to monitor queues. **MF3.4** Use Little's Law. **MF3.5** Gradually eliminate infinite buffers. **MF3.6** Report rudimentary flow efficiency to understand the value of reducing buffers and the leverage of eliminating sources of delay. **MF3.7** Actively close upstream requests that meet the abandonment criteria.
	Core	**MF3.8** Develop triage discipline. **MF3.9** Manage dependencies. **MF3.10** Analyze and report aborted work items. **MF3.11** Use classes of service to affect selection. **MF3.12** Forecast delivery. **MF3.13** Apply qualitative Real Options Thinking.
ML4	Transition	**MF4.1** Collect and report detailed flow efficiency analysis. **MF4.2** Use explicit buffers to smooth flow. **MF4.3** Use two-phase commit for delivery commitment. **MF4.4** Analyze to anticipate dependencies. **MF4.5** Establish refutable versus irrefutable demand.
	Core	**MF4.6** Determine reference class data set. **MF4.7** Forecast using reference classes, Monte Carlo simulations, and other models. **MF4.8** Allocate capacity across swim lanes. **MF4.9** Allocate capacity by color of work item. **MF4.10** Make appropriate use of forecasting. **MF4.11** Assess forecasting models for robustness. **MF4.12** Use statistical methods for decision making.
ML5	Transition	**MF5.1** Utilize hybrid fixed service teams together with a flexible labor pool.
	Core	

Specific Practices Descriptions

Maturity Level 0

MF0.1 Define work types based on nature of tasks.

Description

Categorize work items based on task nature.

Examples of work types:

- For software development: development, maintenance

- For administrative work: accounting, procurement, operations

- For marketing: regular marketing activities, campaigns

- For industry: commercial, design and development, production.

Maturity Level 2

Transition practices

MF2.1 Define work types based on customer requests.

Defining work item types based on customer requests helps to understand the demand patterns of the team's work.

Description

Identify work types taking into consideration the following aspects of the work:

- Customers (source of demand) who may request work; for example, end-users, commercial department, R&D department

- Pattern of work arrival from the identified sources; for example, continuously, random, seasonal (the first week of each month, only a month after delivery)

- Customer expectations (even if unreasonable); for example, resolving doubts, requesting information.

Core practices

MF2.2 Map upstream and downstream flow.

Systems thinking is a way of understanding how a system behaves as a whole rather than through analysis of isolated component parts. [4] It is foundational to the Kanban Method. A key element of the systems thinking approach is mapping the workflow in order to comprehend what it takes to get a work item from "request" to "done." Understanding how the workflow currently functions is essential for identifying appropriate adjustments in order to improve it.

Description

- Sketch the sequence of states though which a type of work evolves from requested (Backlog) to completed (Done).

- Any method is acceptable; some examples are: flowchart, stick man drawing, state chart, or simply listing the states horizontally.

- List the activities that are performed to progress the work item. Use the corresponding verbs for describing them briefly. Avoid the temptation to state which role (who) is responsible for doing a job; instead, focus on what has to be done.

- Designate a column on a kanban board for each state of the workflow.

- When visualizing the workflows for different work types, indicate explicitly which states are not relevant for a particular type; that is, the kanban cards for this type do not stop at this state. As an example, the Bug work items in Figure 37 go directly into the Test Ready column, overpassing the Input Queue and Development columns.

- Refer to VZ2.7 (page 53) for visualizing concurrent activities.

- The upstream states reflect the steps through which ideas or requests go before reaching commitment to be delivered. For example, these are generically *Opportunities – Synthesis – Analysis – Ready to commit.*

Refer to VZ2.12 (page 58) for details on visualizing discovery and delivery workflow.

MF2.3 Manage blocking issues.

Blocked work items contain information that is valuable for improving the flow. Therefore, they have to be treated properly.

Description

- Record and track the reason for which a work item has been blocked. Refer to VZ2.3 for more details about how to visualize blocking issues.

- Treat a blocking issue the same way as the other work items. Namely, assign it an identification number, a title, a team member responsible for the resolution, start and due dates, affected customer-valued work items, and so on.

- Discuss the resolution of the blockages at the daily Kanban Meeting.

- If the team is unable to resolve an issue, it has to be escalated to the appropriate management level or department. (XP2.3, page 122).

- Track blocking issues. This has to be supported by appropriate graphic reports such as bar charts of open and closed issues per period of time, cumulative flow diagram of blockers, root-cause analysis diagrams, and so on.

- Periodically review the types of blocking issues and update the policies for resolving/escalating them (XP2.3, page 122).

MF2.4 Manage defects and other rework types.

Defects are a well-known type of waste. Fixing defects requires additional resources and time that are usually underestimated and therefore cause many adverse effects such as:

- Delays for the project or service they belong to and those that depend on it

- Longer tail in the distribution of lead times and hence poorer predictability of delivery, and a need to start earlier than would otherwise be necessary

- Increased costs

- Assuming some defects escape, reduced value and hence, reduced customer satisfaction

- Reduced value due to opportunity cost of delay while defects were fixed or another rework was performed

- Additional maintenance demand

- Missed business opportunities

Defects are mainly associated with faults in the final product or service. However, there are other types of rework that produce similar effects on product or service delivery. These are, for example, rework of request specifications or product design due to insufficient communication with the customer or other team members, or rework of project plans and reports due to using incomplete or inexact data.

Organizations that are new to managing defects and rework tend not to have explicit policy governing rework. See XP2.4 (page 122) for guidelines about establishing policies for managing defects and other rework types.

Deeper maturity organizations will treat rework as first-class work items and count them against the WIP limit. Excessive rework, then, has the impact of halting the pull of new work until quality issues in current work are resolved.

Description

- Register defects and other rework items.

- Register the reason for the defect or the rework.

- Track rework items for reporting and further analysis.

- Analyze defect and rework data.

- Report rework impact at the Service Delivery Review, Risk Review, and Operations Review.

- Define actions to reduce defects and rework.

Maturity Level 3

Transition practices

MF3.1 Organize around the knowledge discovery process.

An organization is an ecosystem of interdependent services. Visualizing the invisible service work allows organizations to focus on what's important—namely, delivering value to the customer—and manage the system so as to optimize the value delivery.

Description

- For each type of work you develop, map the corresponding workflow (see MF2.2 on page 91).

- Identify the services in your organization, that is, the sequence of nodes on the workflow map that receive input from the predecessor service and deliver output to the successor service according to some criteria. For example, specifying user stories is a service to the software development process. Developing a graphic design is another service to the same process. Making a marketing campaign is service to the entire marketing process.

- Organize knowledge workers around these services and manage the flow of work across them.

Organizing the work around the knowledge discovery phases or the services that compose it and focusing the management on delivering value to the customer instead of on the workers, proves to be an effective management practice and, in addition, causes less resistance to change.

MF3.2 Defer commitment (decide at the "last responsible moment").

Deferring commitment means waiting to decide later. The more frequent cadence of the Replenishment Meeting (FL3.1, page 137), the more deferred commitment is enabled. For example, if we have a weekly replenishment, and we know that a go/no go decision isn't required for another ten days, then we can safely defer a decision until the next Replenishment Meeting. Deferring commitment implies that we should not decide until (1) we are sure we want to do something, (2) we have as much information as possible that may affect the decision to do it or not. However, all options have an expiry date, the point at which it is no longer viable to make a positive choice. The point just prior to that is referred to as the "last responsible moment." Deferring commitment to the last responsible moment brings several benefits:

- Allows keeping options open until the last responsible moment, thus imposing fewer restrictions on the solutions being developed

- Reduces the chances for changes to the requested work or the promised deadline

- Reduces the probabilities of aborting requested work items

- Reduces the overhead for managing modifications, re-prioritization and re-planning

- Reduces the coordination cost for holding meetings

Description

Establish criteria for committing work items, that is, for letting them pass through the commitment point of the kanban system between the pending and in-progress work.

Take into consideration the following aspects of the work items:

- Use a WIP limit: CONWIP, DBR,[4] Cap WIP,[5] or a kanban system. This limits the amount of committed work and forces everything else to remain uncommitted or be actively discarded.

- Develop a comfort level that "deferred" does not imply "never." This is often facilitated by developing explicit policy around the requirements for commitment, also known as the "definition of ready."

- Implement a triage mechanism (see MF3.8) in which, at a regular cadence—usually during the Replenishment Meeting—new work requests are divided into three categories: now; later, and approximately when; and never, that is, discarded.

MF3.3 Use a cumulative flow diagram to monitor queues.

The cumulative flow diagram (CFD, Figure 39) is one of the most useful tools for managing queues. The diagram uses time as its horizontal axis and cumulative quantity as its vertical axis. [4]

---

4. DBR = Drum-Buffer-Rope, the pull-system solution from the Theory of Constraints.
5. Cap WIP is a form of DBR in which the remaining tail of the system following the bottleneck is capped using a CONWIP.

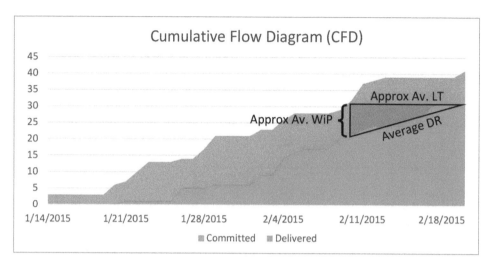

Figure 39   Cumulative Flow Diagram

Description

- Plot the cumulative arrivals at a state of the process on the date on the horizontal axis.

- (Optional) Color the bands to distinguish the amount of work-in-progress in each one of the states.

The vertical distance between the arrival line for the first In-progress state of the kanban system and the departure line for the last In-progress state on a particular date is the work that has been started but not completed yet; that is, the work-in-progress, or the queue size, on that date.

The horizontal distance between the arrival and departure lines shows the average time for a work item to get processed through the system, or the average delivery time.

The slope of the departure line indicates the average capacity of the process to empty the queue, or the average delivery rate.

There are a number of advantages of using CFD:

- To see whether rate of demand (arrivals line) and delivery rate capability (slope of departure line) are in balance

- To understand, when work is getting stuck in the process, if it is due to excess demand or insufficient delivery rate capability

- To become aware of changes in the demand and/or capability patterns

- To recognize emerging bottlenecks (they appear as bulges in the diagram) and their growth rate and be able to act quickly

MF3.4 Use Little's Law.

Little's Law defines the relationship that exists in a stable flow system in which all work items that are selected are delivered. More precisely,

$$\overline{Delivery\ rate} = \frac{\overline{WiP}}{\overline{Lead\ time}}$$

The overline denotes arithmetic mean.

If all the criteria for Little's Law are not met, for example, if there is some abort rate—that is, not all the items that enter the system flow the whole way through and leave—then the equation's prediction will vary from actual observed results by some margin. The larger the digression from the required criteria, the less accurate the results are.

The Little's Law is demonstrated graphically on a Cumulative Flow Diagram (MF3.3).

Description

Use Little's Law for the following purposes:

- Forecast project/service schedule, provided that work items are correctly categorized

- Forecast delivery rates

- Establish WIP limits so as to meet expected delivery time (lead time)

Be aware that Little's Law does not work for unstable kanban systems. Instability would manifest as turbulence in flow or a failure to achieve a stable range of volatility in flow. Unpredictable arrival patterns; large batches of work; or unpredictable flow problems relating to specialists; unavailability of shared resources; delays due to external dependencies; unforeseen circumstances; or an unusual mix of work items, size of work items, or classes of service may cause turbulence. Turbulent systems are unpredictable, and Little's Law is inappropriate under these conditions.

MF3.5 Gradually eliminate infinite buffers.

Buffers are used for many purposes in kanban systems:

- Storing work so that it is instantly available to pull in between replenishment intervals

- Storing work for shared resources normally not instantly available but not capacity constrained

- Storing work between activities in a workflow such that the activities before and after the buffer can operate at their own speed and with their own variability in local cycle times

- Storing work in front of a bottleneck such that the bottleneck will never be idle despite variability in arrival of upstream work

- As a proxy for, or ghost of, work sent to another system or service, either inside the business or external, while the work waits to be completed

- Storing work in front of a batch transfer within the system; the transfer may be triggered by quantity in the buffer or a cadence of time.

Typically, we buffer inputs to the system, outputs from the system, variability between activities within the workflow of the system (chance cause variation), dependencies on external services (assignable cause variation), and bottlenecks.

To couple a series of activities in a workflow into a "pull" system, we need to eliminate infinite buffers (also known as unbounded queues) between the functions. This is done by bracketing an activity and its "done" buffer with a single WIP limit (see also LW3.3). So, we move from a Proto-Kanban aggregated team kanban at ML2 to a full-service delivery workflow kanban at ML3.

To couple dependent services and dependent kanban systems together, we need to eliminate infinite buffers (or unbounded queues) in parking lots, ghosting or proxying the work sent out to another system. This takes us from a network of independently op-erating, locally optimizing services to an interdependent network that is constrained by the slowest moving activity within the slowest service in the network. The consequence of this is achieving true end-to-end pull—from customer commitment to delivery—and predictable service delivery at large scale.

Eliminating infinite buffers (unbounded queues) is a core discipline for achieving smooth flow at large scale.

Description

- Ideally, buffers should be sized to cope with the upper limit of chance-cause varia-tion in the arrival rate of work from upstream. In reality, this quantitative approach is only realistic at ML4 and deeper. At shallower maturity levels it is more likely that an empirical approach to buffer sizing or setting WIP limits for an activity is used.

- Pick a reasonable number, then adjust upward if the downstream system starves frequently due to a lack of "pullable" work from upstream.

- Adjust downward if the buffer is never completely exhausted, even for the briefest amount of time.

The consequence of properly sized buffers is smooth, predictable flow and shorter lead times. Accurate WIP limits and buffer sizing is dependent on the stability of the overall system. If local cycle times fail to exhibit stability, then it will be impossible to establish consistent WIP limits while avoiding occasional starvation of activities or lower flow efficiency while work items wait to be pulled. Stable system capability is a necessary condition for improved efficiency.[6]

MF3.6 Report rudimentary flow efficiency to understand the value of reducing buffers and the leverage of eliminating sources of delay.

$$\overline{Flow\ efficiency} = \frac{\overline{Work\ time}}{\overline{Lead\ time}} \bullet 100\%$$

Flow efficiency is an indicator of waste in the process. More precisely, that the work in-progress spends time waiting. Therefore, decreasing the lead time requires reducing the buffers, which leads to improving the speed and the quality of work.

Description

- Collect the lead time data per work item type and calculate the average.

- Collect the work time data per work item type and calculate the average.
  The work time is the time a work item spends under active processing, independent of how many people work on it. For example, the work time for a surgery is two hours, independent of how many doctors are doing it.

- Calculate the flow efficiency using the above formula.

- Analyze which buffers can be reduced to decrease lead time.

MF3.7 Actively close upstream requests that meet the abandonment criteria.

See XP3.3 (page 124) about defining work request abandonment policies.

Description

- Actively close all upstream requests that meet the criteria of the established policy.

- Periodically analyze the causes for abandoning the options and take appropriate actions, if necessary.

Core practices

MF3.8 Develop triage discipline.

The intent of triage is to avoid overburdening a system as well as providing some rudimentary prioritization or selection and sequencing criteria. Work should be separated into three basic categories: now, later, and never. Items for later may receive some further treatment to establish if not now, then approximately when. Setting expectations with

---

6. A fuller understanding of system stability and its impact is provided in Enterprise Services Planning.

"approximately when" has a psychological benefit in alleviating anxiety over a belief that, "if not now, then never."

With Kanban, triage is mainly applied to the pool of options prior to the commitment point, and specifically to items that are "ready to commit."

Description

- Go through newly arrived items and decide if each should be committed, deferred, or discarded.

- Apply triage periodically to any newly arrived items, typically during a Replenishment Meeting.

- Triage can be simplified, or its impact lessened, by introducing policies such as a guillotine on older items, that is, that items older than a determined time, for example, six months, are automatically discarded.

- Triage is most commonly associated with prioritizing defects for fixing. It can equally be applied to new work requests and blocking-issue management.

MF3.9 Manage dependencies.

Dependencies increase risk. Therefore, their proper visualization and management is important for meeting customer expectations.

See VZ3.5 (page 61) and VZ3.6 (page 62) about visualizing dependencies between work items and using a parking lot to visualize external dependencies, respectively.

Description

The following approaches can be used for managing dependencies:

- Use a separate kanban board for managing dependencies on third parties, such as suppliers, other teams, specialists, or external organizations.

- Plot dependencies on a dependency matrix explicitly indicating the reliance of a work item on other items or teams.

- Periodically analyze the dependence-related blockers. Identify the causes and take actions to prevent them from occurring in the future.

- Have a periodic meeting with representatives of each kanban system regarding communication and resolution of issues relating to dependencies.

- Escalate dependencies that cannot be managed within the service delivery workflow team to the Operations Review.

MF3.10 Analyze and report aborted work items .

Aborted work items have consumed resources without delivering value to the customer. Aborted work usually occurs because commitment was made too early with insufficient information.

Description

- Explicitly identify aborted work items. Collect the tickets that represent them or register them for a subsequent analysis.

- Periodically analyze the causes for aborting work items after the replenishment commitment point.

- Develop an aborted work report.

- Explicitly quantify the impact of the abandoned work.

- Report the aborted work items analysis results at the Service Delivery Review (FL3.4, page 138).

- Through a review at an appropriate level, such as Service Delivery Review, Risk Review, or Operations Review, consider revising policies for "definition of ready" and triage criteria to reduce the future possibility of aborted work.

MF3.11 Use classes of service to affect selection.

In general, any class of service other than first-in, first-out (FIFO) queuing affects flow and adds delivery risk to a kanban system. Classes of service are used to mitigate or react to the business or to other external risks associated with a work item. The more urgent, critical, or valuable an item, the higher its class of service is likely to be. It is a good risk hedging strategy to allocate capacity to classes of service and prevent too many items that are urgent or critical—or both—from entering the system, otherwise the system's routine ability to deliver will be severely affected.

Description

- Decide the capacity distribution per class of service (see Figure 40), for example, using 5% of the available capacity for processing Expedite work items, when necessary, 20% for Fixed Date, 50% for Standard work, and 10% for Intangible.

- Replenish the input queue with work items of classes of service that fit the agreed distribution.

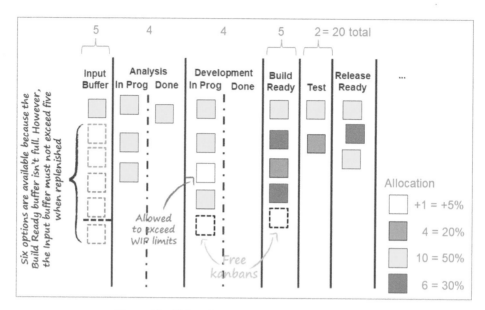

Figure 40   Using classes of service to affect selection

MF3.12 Forecast delivery.

A forecast is a prediction of what will happen in the future. There are two basic types of delivery forecast: forecast when a delivery of a fixed scope of work will be made (*when will it be done?*) and forecast how much work will be delivered on a fixed and known delivery date (*how much can I expect?*). Unlike estimating, which tends to use a reductionist and deterministic approach, forecasting uses a probabilistic, non-deterministic approach. Consequently, forecasting is cheaper, faster, and often more accurate than estimating. We might think of estimating as a white-box approach that requires a lot of analysis and guess work, while forecasting takes a black-box approach that relies on factual historical data to model a probability distribution.

Forecasts are based on an understanding of historical patterns, collection of historical data, and an assumption that system capability and process performance in the near future will continue to reflect the recent past. This is known as the "equilibrium assumption," specifically referring to the concept of a period of equilibrium in the observed capability.

Forecasts should provide a range of probable outcomes. For a fixed scope, a forecast should provide the earliest anticipated date and the latest anticipated date. Ideally, a probability distribution function showing the probability of any specific date within the range should be provided. For a fixed delivery date, a forecast should provide the smallest anticipated scope complete and the largest anticipated scope complete, again, ideally, with a probability distribution function showing the probability of any one outcome within the range.

Forecasts can be made using different sources of input data and using a variety of different mathematical equations or simulation algorithms. With Kanban it is common for people to use Little's Law or the Monte Carlo Simulation to produce forecasts.

Common sources of input for delivery forecasts include delivery rate (or throughput) data, work item lead time data, and local cycle time data for each individual state in a workflow.

Description

- To have confidence in the forecasts, it is important to have a stable and predictable system. The Cumulative Flow Diagram (MF3.3) can easily show the stability of a system with respect to Little's Law. If the arrival rate and the departure rate on the diagram are in sync and the lines are not diverging then the system is stable.

- To forecast the delivery of a single work item, make a histogram of the lead time data for its type, and class of service, if appropriate, then report a percentile that you feel comfortable with, for example, the eighty-fifth percentile. The lead time indicated at the eighty-fifth percentile suggests a six out of seven chance of delivering on or before that date.

- If the kanban system is stable, use Little's Law for forecasting (MF3.4). Little's Law is a function of averages, and therefore it can only forecast average (mean) outcomes, not a range. It requires that its input data exhibit a Gaussian distribution. A kanban system is stable if it is devoid of turbulence and exhibits a defined range of volatility for delivery rate and/or lead times.

- Make a Scatterplot diagram of the lead time for a type of work and take, for example, the eighty-fifth percentile.

- Subtract the obtained delivery time estimate from the expected delivery time. If a work item is started before this point in time, there is an eighty-five percent or better chance of it being delivered on time. Otherwise, the chance of delivering on time is getting smaller.

- Simulations can be run using throughput data for an entire system, with a granularity of each day or week of system operation. This is a rather coarse, or crude, simulation with low fidelity. A higher fidelity simulation might simulate the movement of every ticket on a kanban board by randomly estimating the local cycle time each ticket spends in each state in the workflow.

- At deeper maturity levels, forecasts should be delivered with an explanation of the method used and an assessment of its robustness. The robustness of the forecasting method is an indicator of the trustworthiness or confidence that can be given to the prediction.

MF3.13 Apply qualitative Real Options Thinking.

General literature on Real Options Theory describes it as the application of financial option theory to real-world problems. It often goes further and describes it as the application of the option pricing algorithm for which the economists Black, Merton and Scholes won the Nobel Prize in Economics, to such real world problems.

However, there is a much simpler notion of real options, or just options, thinking. To have options is to have choices. So, a qualitative understanding of real options means that there is explicit recognition of choices and a decision to discard a choice or pursue it by investing further. Simple analogies can be drawn to examples such as picking a spouse. There is a progression from mixing socially with several prospects to dating exclusively, resulting in a discard or escalate decision. Escalation may involve engagement or moving in together. Further time may go by and again a discard or escalate decision occurs involving marriage. Later there may be a decision about whether to start a family. And so on.

Each of these decision points, where there is either a discard or an increased investment to develop the option further, represents an embedded option.

Chris Matts and Olav Maassen, in their wider work on risk management and specifically in their book *Commitment*, have provided a lot of valuable guidance on qualitative assessment and the use of Real Options Theory. Their aphorism

"Options have value. Options Expire. Never decide early unless you know why."

is just one example of how skills in option theory can be developed without a need for a quantitative mathematical understanding.

Real Options Theory relates directly to deferred commitment—never decide early unless you know why—and the general concept of commitment, choice, and triage. For organizations adopting Kanban where there is some basic capability in triage, deferred commitment and an understanding of the meaning of commitment and its implications, developing knowledge, experience, and capability with Real Options Theory is the next step in deeper and more powerful risk management.

A qualitative understanding of Real Options Theory encourages the emergence of questions like when should we decide? and how much should we invest before we reach a decision point? "When should we decide" suggests defining the last responsible moment or understanding the expiry date of an option (or choice). "How much should we invest?" suggests emergence of a skill in option pricing. A qualitative understanding of Real Options Theory is a natural evolutionary step toward a quantitative understanding. However, it has value in and of itself. A qualitative understanding may be a skill that can become pervasive and democratized across the wider workforce, while a more advanced quantitative understanding may be the niche for specialist risk analysts. A broad understanding of options theory across a workforce will enable much more advanced risk management decisions at deeper maturity levels. The workforce will understand why a decision was made, even if they don't understand the precise details. Developing a broad understanding of options theory is an enabler of deeper maturity, optimizing behavior. It enables unity and alignment behind decisions, and it provides language to frame decisions and achieve consensus and agreement. Triage becomes more effective with a workforce skilled in qualitative real options assessment.

Maturity Level 4

Transition practices

MF4.1 Collect and report detailed flow efficiency analysis.

Flow efficiency is the metric that measures the percentage of time a work item or kanban board ticket spends in valuable, value-adding activities versus its total lead time.

$$\overline{Flow\ efficiency} = \frac{\overline{Work\ time}}{Lead\ time} \bullet 100\%$$

Description

Maturity level 4 organizations look for higher fidelity and greater accuracy of collected data. They analyze it to improve economic results mainly through two things:

- Earlier delivery avoids cost of delay.

- Shorter lead time improves optionality; hence, better flow efficiency improves optionality upstream and enables greater deferred commitment, and potentially lower WIP in the system.

To collect flow efficiency, it is necessary to have each state in the workflow identified and labeled as a work state or a wait state. Ideally, if it is work state, identify the quantity of multitasking or time-slicing happening to work in that state. For example, a ticket may spend three days in a work state but if the worker was multitasking across three items, then the ticket probably only received around one day of work rather than three days. Because of this problem, most software solutions tend to overstate flow efficiency. They tend to report the full amount of time spent in activity states and credit it all as value-adding work. This is almost never true and hence, current state of the art in reporting flow efficiency is generous in nature.

Time spent in each state must be recorded. This can be done manually. For example, place dots or pins next to a ticket for each day it remains in a column on a kanban board (its state in the workflow) and when it moves, count the dots or pins and record the number. This procedure is repeated for each column on the board and for every ticket on the board. Software systems simply timestamp when a ticket enters and leaves a given state, and the time spent in that state can be calculated by subtracting one from another. Some adjustment for the percentage of the twenty-four-hour calendar day spent working may be desirable. For example, there may be a default that no "day" is longer than eight hours. At the time of writing, it is not known how effective commercial software packages are at calculating and reporting flow efficiency. However, regardless of accuracy, they are at least consistent from one ticket to the next and useful for relative comparison within the same workflow, service, or kanban board. It is, however, dangerous to compare flow efficiency metrics across organizations or to try and use them for benchmarking or comparative assessment. It is not recommended at this time to use flow efficiency as an Organizational Process Performance tool at CMMI ML4.[7]

MF4.2 Use explicit buffers to smooth flow.

Description

Bottlenecks and shared resources (or non-instant availability resources or services) impact and impede flow. Flow can be smoothed by placing an explicit buffer in front of a bottleneck or non-instant availability shared resource or service. The sizing of the buffer must be treated differently for each case.

In the case of a bottleneck, the buffer is placed in front of it, in order to prevent the bottleneck from starving. The buffer just upstream of the bottleneck is intended to hold work so that there is always something available to the bottleneck, that it remains fully exploited, and is operating at maximum utilization. This maximizes the throughput, or delivery rate, of work through the system. It also avoids upstream activities from stalling because of a lack of downstream kanban at or just before the bottleneck. The buffer smooths flow upstream while maximizing throughput of the service and its end-to-end workflow.

Buffers should be sized such that potential variability in cycle times upstream, or variability of cycle time in the bottleneck, never creates a situation in which the bottleneck will be without work.

For example, imagine a bottleneck with a local cycle time of 0.25 days to 1.0 days, with an average of 0.5 days, or a throughput of 2.0 work items per day. The upstream function has a cycle time of 0.2 days to 0.8 days, with an average of 0.4 days, or a throughput potential of 2.5 per day. However, the upstream function has a series of quite long or large items and in the past two days has only produced one item, with another half-finished and due to be pullable by the bottleneck mid-day tomorrow. Meanwhile, the bottleneck has been running quickly and has produced six items in the past two days. This was possible because the buffer in front of the bottleneck contained at least five items that were pullable and had already completed the previous upstream step.

---

7. We know of a large organization, a telecoms equipment vendor, that has deployed Kanban across tens of thousands of employees and many product and business units and is actively using flow efficiency as an organizational process performance measure and benchmarking tool. This organization has the advantage that they built their own tool and it is used ubiquitously as the standard across the entire organization, and that kanban is only deployed in software and hardware development and testing and not in many other professional services functions such as marketing or back office functions such as finance or human resources.

While it is technically possible to calculate buffer sizes mathematically, the more pragmatic approach is empirical adjustment. Create the buffer as part of the workflow design and select a starting kanban limit, say three. If the bottleneck suffers idleness, then adjust it upward. If the buffer never runs dry, or empties for just a short time, then it is probably too large, so adjust it downward. Such adjustments may be necessary for several weeks until a stable operating value is reached.

Sizing a buffer in front of a non-instant availability resource or service is perhaps easier. First, ask how often is the resource available? For example, daily. And for how long is the availability? For example, one hour per day. Now ask, what is the maximum reasonable throughput in one hour? Throughput or delivery rate data tend to be Gaussian distributed. For example, two to eight items, with a mean of four. The distribution will have a skewed bell curve. If we were to choose a buffer size of eight, we should be completely safe. However, this might result in turning the non-instant availability, shared resource into a bottleneck. Perhaps a size of six or seven is better. Once again, empirical adjustment is the most pragmatic approach. Start with a reasonable number and adjust. If your shared resource is underutilized, then increase the buffer size. If your shared resource is unable to empty the buffer during a period of availability, then reduce the buffer size.

MF4.3 Use two-phase commit for delivery commitment.

Description

The term *two-phase commit*, with respect to kanban systems, refers to breaking out the commitment to do something with the specific commitment to deliver on a particular date. Analogously, it is compared to the act of becoming engaged versus the wedding ceremony. Engagement to be married is a commitment to marry. It is a commitment to proceed. However, it is extremely rare for the wedding day already to be set and planned at the point of the engagement. Hence, the act of getting married involves a two-phase commitment. First, the promise to marry, followed, on the day of the wedding, by the actual commitment to marry.

Using two- or multi-phase commitments is a means to manage customer expectations. It is popular with, for example, furniture retailers, who rarely keep stock on hand and have to order items from a warehouse or manufacturer. They often promise only vague delivery dates, such as ten to thirteen weeks, and then, as the delivery gets closer and more certain, they add precision to their forecast and their promise—your dining table will be delivered in week thirty-one. Then later they'll say that your dining table is scheduled for delivery on Tuesday of week thirty-one, and finally, perhaps a day or two prior, that the delivery truck will arrive with your dining table between eleven a.m. and one p.m. on Tuesday.

Kanban systems and practitioners have benefited from similar approaches to managing customer expectations. Selection of an item at a Replenishment Meeting is a commitment to do the work and deliver the finished item. However, there is no commitment as to when. After the item is some of the way across the board, (Figure 41), and there is greater certainty around the remaining lead time, a specific delivery date (the second phase of the commitment) may be communicated. From that point on, the item in-progress has a fixed delivery date, and effectively a slightly higher class of service, to ensure that the commitment is met.

Psychologically, two-phase commit has an advantage: it makes it far more likely that an item will be delivered against a specific promise of delivery. A single commitment to both undertake the work and make delivery on a given day or within a specified period is fragile: there is a greater probability of late delivery and a broken promise. Hence, use of a two-phase commitment enables a service to be seen as much more trustworthy from the customer's perspective.

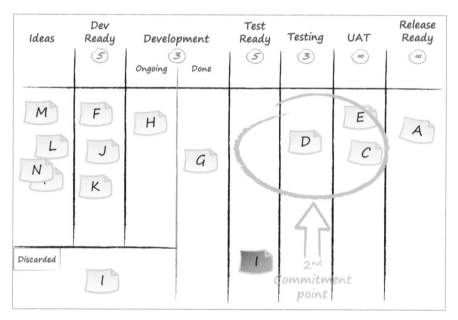

Figure 41   Visualizing the approximate position of tickets before the second phase of commitment with a defined delivery date is made

MF4.4 Analyze to anticipate dependencies.

Will a work request produce additional knock-on requests of other services? Being able to anticipate dependent demand and schedule it in advance may improve predictability and inform commitment. Without analysis to inform whether a dependency is likely, the network of services—our system of systems—is operating in a purely reactionary fashion.

Unplanned, unscheduled, or unanticipated dependent demand is likely to lead to longer lead times, less predictability, poorer timeliness, and less fit-for-purpose service delivery. It is hard to maintain deeper maturity behavior in a purely reactionary mode of operation.

Description

There are two forms of analysis to establish if a dependent request is likely or necessary—the probabilistic approach and the deterministic approach.

The probabilistic approach is fast and cheap and therefore preferred. However, it gives us a mere probability of whether a dependency exists and may result in some sub-optimal behavior when we guess one way and the result goes the other way. For example, if we believe there is a low probability of a dependency and so ignore that chance, and then the dependent request emerges later, our system or network of services has to react to late-breaking information.

With the probabilistic approach, historical data for this type of work is analyzed for whether it spawned dependent requests in the past. Historical data is used to predict the future. If, for example, every second ticket has historically needed a dependency, then there is a fifty percent chance that this ticket will generate one.

For example, we run an advertising agency and one of our services is to design ad campaigns. When a customer requests a campaign, what is the probability that the campaign will generate a need for custom photography rather than use stock images?

The deterministic approach involves business analysis, systems analysis, and decomposition of the request into a likely design in order to assess what additional services may be needed. For example, will the new features in our investment banking application require API changes to our trading platform? We can "determine" this through analysis and design work. This deterministic approach isn't foolproof. Business and systems analysis is never perfect, and designs tend to change during implementation. So, there is still a probabilistic element to our determinism. We may believe that our analysis and design says there is a dependency, but historically, this analysis has been only eighty-five percent accurate. So, even the expensive and time-consuming deterministic approach merely gives us a confidence level and won't eliminate changes and operating in reactionary mode altogether.

As a general rule, we want to use the probabilistic approach where it is most effective and accurate and the deterministic approach only when the impact and costs of a mistake are severe. For example, if failing to detect the need for an API change in our trading platform caused a delay in deployment of our new investment banking application, and due to the regulatory nature of that industry, we missed a deadline for new legal requirements and suffered a denial of trade, then the consequences of failing to detect the dependency were severe. As a result, we may prefer to start earlier, invest time and money in deterministically analyzing whether a dependency exists, and have far greater confidence in our planning.

MF4.5 Establish refutable versus irrefutable demand.

Description

Refutable, or discretionary, demand means that requests for work can be refuted, denied, or declined. As they are discretionary, the service provider is not obliged to accept them. Discretionary work is optional work, and the requests for it represent real options in an upstream or Discovery Kanban workflow. Discretionary work is work that can be discarded at triage. If it is possible to triage a work request into the category of "won't do it," "never," or "no," then the work is discretionary and refutable.

Irrefutable work is not discretionary. There is no option to decline it. A full triage decision is not possible. Only the options of "now" or "later" exist with irrefutable work.

Work is irrefutable because it is already committed, and the decision to commit to it was made by someone else, somewhere else, often at a much higher pay grade.

Irrefutable demand represents a problem because it is often a source of overburdening and hence, a root cause of disappointment and service delivery that isn't fit-for-purpose.

Irrefutable demand can also be of a legal or regulatory nature and hence, if we committed to being in that line of business, then we must abide by laws and regulations in the territories in which we operate. Meeting such demand is table stakes for entering the market. At the point of service delivery, the work is irrefutable.

Other irrefutable demand can happen because a feature, function, component, sub-system, or system is table stakes and is required for a fit-for-purpose design. For example, a car must have wheels and tires. If we are in the business of designing and manufacturing cars, then we must include wheels and tires and the request for them isn't refutable.

The final category of irrefutable demand is that it is mission critical. For example, if we are an ecommerce trading house and our web site crashes, then the request to repair it and bring it back to full operation is irrefutable—such a request is related to our mission. We cannot trade on the World Wide Web without a website.

In general, demand directly related to the identity of our business—our why—our vision, mission, and purpose for existence—is irrefutable.

However, there is often a perception of irrefutability when, in fact, the work is refutable. Or the irrefutable work still has some elasticity or fungibility to its definition. Perceived irrefutable demand is often something that can be challenged. The first step in challenging it is to identify it. List it. Measure it. Assess its impact.

If previously perceived irrefutable demand can be challenged and its irrefutability changed or modified in terms of fidelity or timeliness, then we have an opportunity to better manage flow.

Core practices

MF4.6 Determine reference class data set.

Where simulation algorithms are used to forecast future outcomes and the algorithm relies on a bootstrap data set selected from historical observations, it is important that the policies for selecting the reference class data set are made explicit.

Description

The policies for selecting the reference data set for the bootstrap of the simulation algorithm should be made explicit. These policies can be assessed to demonstrate the robustness of the forecasting model (see MF4.11 on page 114).

Ideally, a reference class data set is extracted from a period of equilibrium, a period without turbulence. Where the historical data set—the run series or the time series—does not exhibit stability (has no period without turbulence), then the use of reference class forecasting and bootstrap data for simulation algorithms is not mathematically valid (see MF4.10).

MF4.7 Forecast using reference classes, Monte Carlo simulations, and other models.

Description

Simulation algorithms can be used to forecast outcomes and answer questions such as

- How long will it take to complete this batch of work (or project)?

- How many work items will be completed by a given date in the future?

Simulations require parametric probability distribution functions derived from a "best fit" to historical data patterns, or a simple bootstrap reference data set. Simplistically, a reference data set might be "the last thirty data points."

Whether the simulation uses a parametric function or a bootstrap data set should be declared. The model error and simulation error can then be assessed. Model error refers to how well the parametric function "fits" or resembles the actual historically observed data. Simulation error refers to gaps in the bootstrap data set in comparison to a close fit parametric function. Such gaps represent values that will never occur in the simulation while they almost certainly will occur in real life, and hence, their absence produces simulation errors. (See FL 4.3, Assess the robustness of a forecasting model or algorithm.)

In the Kanban community it is widely held that bootstrap algorithms are more pragmatic—it is easy to acquire historical data to bootstrap a simulation—and that the simulation error is generally not greater than any model error would be if a "best fit" parametric probability distribution function were selected instead.

MF4.8 Allocate capacity across swim lanes.

Description

A WIP limit is indicated on each row of a kanban board. Active work-in-progress in that row (or lane) of the board should not exceed the limit indicated.

This approach creates a pull system per row of the board. The work pulled through that row may be of a specific work item type, class of service, or other risk. The choice of type or risk of work to place in the row is a separate design choice from the capacity allocation indicated by a WIP limit for the row.

MF4.9 Allocate capacity by color of work item.

Description

A WIP limit is indicated in a legend at the side of the board. For each color of ticket, a kanban limit is set. Active work-in-progress of each color should not exceed the limit indicated.

This approach creates a pull system per color. The meaning of the color referring to class of service, work type, or other risk is independent of this simple capacity allocation by ticket color.

MF4.10 Make appropriate use of forecasting.

Description

The appropriateness and applicability of models, mathematical equations, and statistical techniques should be known and understood and the use of such models should be appropriate in context.

For example, the popular Little's Law equation from queuing theory, which states that the average delivery rate is equal to the average work-in-progress divided by the average lead time, is a function of averages—each of the three algebraic components is an average. Little's Law was conceived in a domain where distribution of data points is assumed to be Gaussian in nature. This underlying assumption makes the use of the arithmetic mean an appropriate choice, and in domains where the spread of the bell curve, the alpha, is relatively low, then very few data points are required to use Little's Law to forecast an outcome in the near future with acceptable accuracy.

As soon as the data set available, such as that for the lead time, is not Gaussian in nature, rather it is super exponential—it resembles a Weibull function with a shape parameter $1.0 < k < 2.0$, then more data points are required for the arithmetic mean to be meaningful and a reasonable assumption. Hence, Little's Law is less effective over short time horizons. It is still useful when projecting seventy to one hundred data points into the future.

If the data set for lead time falls below exponential, exhibiting a Weibull function with shape parameter k < 1.0, then convergence to the arithmetic mean within a reasonable error margin is unlikely for at least 2,000 to 10,000 data points. For all practical purposes, Little's Law is not appropriate or useful as a forecasting tool under these circumstances.

Lead time distributions with long fat tails, where the data set resembles a Weibull function with shape, kappa, k < 1.0, are common in IT operations and other IT services and in any domain with excessive numbers of dependencies on other services, especially if these are external to the organization.

Shallow maturity organizations tend to use mathematical models such as Little's Law blindly and fail to understand when it lets them down. This type of usage is superstitious and tends to lead to a belief that the equation is magical. When it works, all is well and when it doesn't, there may be an emotional reaction resulting in discarding the practice. Deeper maturity organizations understand when it is appropriate to use a model such as Little's Law and apply it in correct situations while deploying alternative techniques in others.

Develop a basic capability to analyze and understand data sets and probability distribution functions (PDFs) that are in one of five data distribution domains:

- Gaussian (Weibull, 2.0 <= k <= 4.0)

    o Also known as mediocristan[8]

- Super-Exponential (Weibull, 1.0 < k < 2.0)

- Exponential (Weibull, k = 1.0)

- Sub-Exponential (Weibull 0.5 < k < 1.0)

- Pareto (fat tailed power laws)

    o Also known as "extremistan"[9]

Select forecasting tools, statistical models, simulation algorithms, and quantitative analysis that is appropriate for each of these data distribution domains. For example, the concept known as the Lindy Effect[10] for predicting the life expectancy of for example a current product, based on its previous period of survival, an ability which relies on a decreasing hazard/mortality rate and an assessment of its health (e.g., its "fitness-for-purpose") is appropriate in a Pareto distributed domain for nonperishable tangible or nontangible goods, such as life expectancy of a Broadway musical, or the career of a pop star.[11] Making

---

8. Nassim Nicholas Taleb, *The Black Swan.*
9. Nassim Nicholas Taleb, *The Black Swan.*
10. https://en.wikipedia.org/wiki/Lindy_effect
11. Note: The career of a pop star, or group, can exceed the actual lifetime of the individual(s); e.g., Elvis Presley, John Lennon, Michael Jackson.

a Lindy Effect assumption/forecast in a domain with Gaussian distributed life expectancy, due to the perishable nature of the entity, would be inappropriate.

Deep maturity organizations should be able to provide a defensible mathematical analysis for their choices of forecasting models.

MF4.11 Assess forecasting models for robustness.

Description

Models and simulation algorithms for forecasting should be subjected to sensitivity analysis and the limits of usefulness of the model or simulation should be understood and defined.

There are some anomalies or dichotomies inherent in mathematics. When quantitative mathematical models are in use, it is important to know their limits or their sensitivity to unexpected input data. For example,

- Models that assume Gaussian distributed data sets are highly sensitive to the assumption of the alpha (or spread in the bell curve) within the data. To have a high level of confidence in the alpha, it is necessary to have a large data set—perhaps 1,000 to 2,000 data points. Where a small number of data points is available, say thirty, and the data is known to be from a domain that is typically Gaussian distributed, then it is dangerous to make assumptions about the precise nature of the distribution—its mean, median, and mode values—and its spread (or alpha). Derivative conclusions, such as a reasonable number of data points required to create convergence to a mean, that is, how many data points are required to provide a meaningful result for the Central Limit Theorem, may be even more misleading.

- Models that assume Pareto distributed data sets are actually quite robust—just a few random data points, five to ten, may be all that is required to define a good enough model. However, with Pareto distributions, the concept of a mean is a meaningless or useless notion.

- Monte Carlo simulations that rely on Gaussian distributed data sets actually require large numbers of data points to provide forecasts with a high confidence level, while the same simulation algorithm used in a different domain exhibiting a Pareto distributed data set would provide a high-confidence forecast with very few data points.

Mathematical sensitivity analysis for forecasting equations and simulations should be performed and reported on against the expected nature of data in the domain. New data arriving should be continually analyzed to see whether it falls within expected ranges and whether the emerging data set falls within a reasonable variance of the distribution function used in the forecast equation or simulation.

One emerging technique is continual reforecasting, using all new data as it arrives, to build up a set of real data used in bootstrapping a discrete (rather than parametric) simulation. This provides useful insights for robustness and sensitivity analysis. For example, what did our forecast tell us about a possible range of delivery dates for our project before we started the project versus what our forecast is telling us now that we have completed half of the project work? By analyzing how the forecasted range of completion dates has changed, the robustness of the original forecast can be assessed.

However, there is a need to understand the stability of the system, and therefore, the validity of simulation from the actual received data. If the data set exhibits turbulence, also known as volatility of volatility, then the actual data cannot be considered a stable reference class data set from which to forecast future outcomes. More mature models will take this into account.

Statistical models can also be assessed for other behavioral attributes. For example, a model that assumes its input data is a small random sample from a bigger data population, for example, seven random data points from a set of 2,000 will be sensitive to the randomness of the sample as well as to the number of random samples. If the real-world situation is that we don't have a random sample from a larger data population—in fact, all we have is the first seven data points—then any model we use will be exposed to the risk that the first seven data points are not representative of the entire data population.

Use of statistical quantitative models without thorough sensitivity and robustness analysis is likely to result in shallow maturity results—low predictability, and actual outcomes at unreasonable or unfit levels of variance from original predictions. Use of statistical methods can provide a veneer of deeper maturity when in fact it is merely misdirection. The existence of statistical models and quantitative analysis is in itself not an indicator of a deep maturity organization. Deep maturity organizations are typically capable of delivering against both customer and economic expectations. This practice of assessing models in use for robustness and sensitivity is an important component of competent quantitative management.

MF4.12 Use statistical methods for decision making.

Description

Adopt the use of statistical mathematic models and analysis in order to make decisions.

For example, a customer desires delivery within sixty days. What is the probability that we can meet the customer's expectation and deliver on or before their expected due date?

If this question is answered through statistical analysis of historical data used to create a lead time histogram or approximate, "best fit" parametric probability distribution function (PDF), then quantitative decision making is present.

For example, if recent historical data suggests it is eighty percent probable that we can meet the sixty-day delivery expectation, we have a four in five chance of meeting expectations and being seen as "fit-for-purpose." A risk-management decision can now be made regarding whether the twenty percent chance of failing to meet this customer's expectations is worth taking. A decision one way or another will likely be highly influenced by the consequences of late delivery. If the consequences are severe, such as a "denial of trade" restriction from a regulating authority, then we may choose to pass on the request and exit that business, or we may choose to provide a higher class of service to accelerate the development and reduce the lead time. If the consequences are minor, such as an uncomfortable meeting with senior leaders from the customer's organization, we may choose to carry the risk and suffer the consequences.

The fact that an informed decision was based on objective statistical analysis of probability and impact is the key behavior expected at maturity level 4.

Maturity Level 5

Core practices

MF5.1 Utilize hybrid fixed service teams together with a flexible labor pool.

Description

Labor pool (or staffing) liquidity is an important attribute for minimizing delay and maintaining smooth flow. The kanban board design pattern illustrated in VZ5.1 provides the visualization of this concept. Small teams providing a single or limited range of services are organizationally merged into a larger group offering a much wider range of services (servicing a great number of work item types).

Each service offered occupies a lane on the board. Approximately half of the workforce from this merged larger group is allocated as a fixed service team, to undertake work of the types intended for that row on the board. One member of the team will be designated as the service delivery manager and carries the accountability and responsibility for taking the customer's order, accepting the work, making commitment to delivery, managing the flow, and ensuring delivery occurs.

The remaining half of the larger group workforce are not allocated to specific services. They represent a floating pool of labor available to do any work for which they have the skills. This floating pool of labor can be used to augment any one of the fixed service teams. These workers are given avatars for the board and the avatar is placed to show where they are currently working, which service they are assisting.

The labor pool liquidity pattern provides an advantage when there is ebb and flow in demand for any specific work item type or service offered, and where there may be limited resources and availability for specialist skills and a specialist can't be embedded in each individual service team. The labor pool liquidity pattern helps improve staff utilization at times when they might otherwise be underutilized due to an ebb in demand for the type of work their team services.

Aggregating teams together into larger multi-service groups, with a floating labor pool, is a means to improve both effectiveness and efficiency and to optimize the performance of the organization. Empirical observations suggest that this pattern works at the following scale: four to six small teams merged into one multi-service group offering six to eight services; with a total of twenty to forty staff, split into one floating labor pool representing forty to sixty percent of the total staff, while each dedicated service team consists of a minimum of two staff members and often three or four.

An advanced version of this practice will also incorporate an explicit career development path. New hires, essentially apprentices, will enter as team members on one fixed service team. After an agreed period, these junior members will be rotated to another fixed service team. This pattern will repeat until they've worked in all of the different services. At this point, these apprentices have acquired all of the skills and experience necessary to work as part of the floating labor pool. They are now eligible for a switch to the floating pool, with a promotion and pay grade increase. The floating labor pool are journeymen workers who have all the skills and experience required to be effective assisting on any of the services.

From time to time, new service delivery managers will be required to lead fixed service teams. A floating labor pool worker asked to take a service delivery manager role should be given a promotion and a pay raise. Service delivery managers carry accountability and responsibility for the service delivery capability of their team. They are also responsible and accountable for the development of new junior personnel obtaining experience working on the team as part of their rotation and journey toward promotion to the floating labor pool. For these additional responsibilities, the service delivery manager position should carry additional status and remuneration acknowledging the additional responsibilities.

8 | Make Policies Explicit

Goal

Establish clear rules for managing work that allow for developing a better understanding of the entire process and improving it further with consensus.

Benefits

- Establishes explicit criteria for making decisions related to work items and process
- Establishes criteria and guidelines for managing risks
- Manages dependencies
- Aligns strategy and capability

Specific Practices Summary

Maturity Level		Make Policies Explicit (XP) Practice
ML0	Core	**XP0.1** Define personal kanban policies.
ML1	Transition	
	Core	**XP1.1** Define initial policies.
ML2	Transition	**XP2.1** Define initial services. **XP2.2** Elaborate further policies.
	Core	**XP2.3** Define blocking issue escalation policies. **XP2.4** Define policies for managing defects and other rework types.
ML3	Transition	**XP3.1** Establish explicit purpose of metrics. **XP3.2** Establish initial request acceptance policies. **XP3.3** Define work request abandonment policies. **XP3.4** Establish replenishment commitment point.
	Core	**XP3.5** Establish pull criteria. **XP3.6** Establish a delivery commitment point. **XP3.7** Establish customer acceptance criteria for each work item or a class of work items. **XP3.8** Define classes of service.
ML4	Transition	**XP4.1** Explicitly define fitness-for-purpose, and manage based on metrics.
	Core	**XP4.2** Establish demand shaping policies. **XP4.3** Establish SLA on dependent services.
ML5	Transition	
	Core	**XP5.1** Align strategy and capability.

Specific Practices Descriptions

Maturity Level 0

Core practices

XP0.1 Define personal kanban policies.

Description

The intent of the personal kanban policies is to make it easier for an individual to organize her work and conduct it with less stress.

The personal kanban policies typically include the following:

- A limit on the in-progress work (LW0.1, page 83)

- A cadence for making a personal reflection (see FL0.1, page 134)

Maturity Level 1

Core practices

XP1.1 Define initial policies.

Policies define rules to be applied during process execution. They govern the behavior of the individuals and teams. Therefore, it is important to set them up with consensus and respect them.

Description

Together with the team members, define the initial policies to be used for guiding the process. They typically address the following aspects:

- Per-person WIP limits
- Team WIP limits
- Conditions at which WIP limits may be exceeded
- Frequency and criteria for replenishing the Next column
- Cadence of the Kanban Meeting
- Other rules guiding decision making

Maturity Level 2

Transition practices

XP2.1 Define initial services.

Description

Work flows through different activity phases, visualized as stages on the delivery kanban board (VZ2.4, page 52).

For each activity, there is a customer or another activity that provides the necessary input, as well as a following activity or a customer who receives the outcome. Therefore, from a service-orientation perspective, the chain of activity phases can be seen as a sequence of services instead of functions or specializations in the organization.

Taking this approach implies that the entire chain of services must be taken into consideration and managed as a whole in order to improve the flow of value to the end customers.

XP2.2 Elaborate further policies.

Removing ambiguity from the environment encourages deeper maturity and moves the organization toward more desirable business outcomes.

Description

Extend the policies defined in XP1.1 (page 121) with the following aspects:

- Cadence of the internal team Replenishment Meeting
- Activity-based WIP limits
- Defined constraints on work item size
- Definitions of the work item sizes
- Criteria for "done" for the board columns
- How to visualize blocked work items

Normally, a policy should be in place that directs the team to resolve blocking issues before pulling new work to the system, that is, a blocked item still counts against the WIP limit. Organizations often temporarily remove blocked items from the WIP limit. This typically results in an accumulation of unresolved blocked issues, which slows down the flow.

Core practices

XP2.3 Define blocking issue escalation policies.

Resolving blockages is key for improving flow of work, reducing both delays and rework.

Description

- Define what kind of blocking issues can be resolved autonomously by the teams.
- Define what kind of blocking issues have to be escalated to what organizational role and by what means.
- The policy for escalating issues has to be agreed on collaboratively by all departments at the organizational level, and it must be documented.
- Periodically revise the policy based on an understanding of the type of blocking issues that occur (MF2.3, page 92).

XP2.4 Define policies for managing defects and other rework types.

Description

A policy is required for whether a rework ticket should be attached to the work item that spawned it and hence, remain in the same work state (e.g., *Test*) where the problem was discovered, or whether it should be sent backward to the column of the activity that needs to be reworked (e.g., *Design*).

Keeping rework tickets attached to its parent has the effect of "stop the line" and contributes to the implementation of the Toyota Production System concept of *Jidoka*. This is generally only seen in maturity level 4 or 5 implementations. At maturity level 2, it is typical that the rework ticket is sent backward, and often it doesn't count against the WIP limit. Changing and improving this policy is evidence of deepening maturity.

Maturity Level 3

Transition practices

XP3.1 Establish explicit purpose of metrics.

For each metric or measure recorded and reported, there should be an explicit purpose detailing why the metric is captured and how it is used; that is, what decisions and actions might be expected based on changes in the reported data.

Description

- It may be helpful, though not expected, at ML3 for the metrics to be classified using the Fit-for-Purpose Framework. Each metric should be classified as a Fitness Criteria (for a specific customer purpose) and hence a Key Performance Indicator (KPI), General Health Indicator, Improvement Driver, or Vanity Metric.

- For each fitness criterion, there should be a threshold level that indicates fitness and potentially a second threshold that represents exceeding expectations and over-serving.

  Note: Achieving such a level may not be bad, as the new level of performance may enable a new market segment and new customer purposes. (See Strategy Review, FL5.1.)

- For each general health indicator, there should be an indication of a trading range within which the system would be considered healthy—effectively upper and lower bounds that would signal an intervention and action to be taken.

- For each improvement driver, there should be a target. Achieving the target should trigger switching off the improvement driver and ending the improvement initiative, though often improvement drivers become general health indicators with bounds that may prompt action to investigate why a former improvement action is no longer working, in turn creating demand for a new improvement initiative and an appropriate improvement driver metric.

- Vanity metrics can be formally documented, perhaps with some indication of the social, or emotional, need for the metric. In general, there should be no targets, no ideal trading range, no thresholds, and no goals associated with a vanity metric.

XP3.2 Establish initial request acceptance policies.

Reducing service delivery time allows for more time in the discovery (upstream) part of the workflow. Shorter lead times for delivery improve optionality. Commitment can be deferred until later and consequently risk is better managed.

If a work item goes through the first commitment point, this means that the customer is committed to accept the requested work and the team is committed to delivering it quickly.

Establishing explicit policies for accepting requests facilitates the process of deciding which options to pull in the ready-to-start stage of the delivery kanban system.

Description

- Decide what information about the customer request has to be provided before initiating the delivery process. The following criteria about the request are typically used:
  - o Complete
  - o Clear
  - o Coherent with other requests
  - o Testable
  - o Defined acceptance criteria
- Make sure that enough capacity is available to commit to delivering the work item within the expected time.

XP3.3 Define work request abandonment policies.

In low maturity organizations, it is common for submitted work requests to linger without attention for months or even years. There is never enough capability to get all of the work done. Acknowledging this fact is significant progress. It is useful to create explicit policy to actively close aged work requests that are effectively abandoned and will never be undertaken.

Description

Facilitate a conversation with customers and other stakeholders to determine how old a request must be before it would be considered abandoned. Define this policy explicitly. Refer to MF3.7 for more details about closing out aged work items that meet the criteria.

XP3.4 Establish a replenishment commitment point.

Work items are said to be committed when there is a strong expectation, shared with the customer, that work on them should now proceed to delivery. [7]

The point in the process at which the transition between uncommitted and committed states occurs, typically as result of a Replenishment Meeting (FL3.1, page 137), is referred to as the replenishment commitment point. On a kanban board, this is represented by a line between columns.

There may be a second commitment point later in the process, the point at which the decision to release, deliver, or deploy work items, singly or in batches, is made (FL3.3, page 138).

Description

- Decide the point in the kanban system at which work is committed. This point has to be agreed with the customer as well.

- Define criteria for committing work, that is, work items that pass through the commitment point. Refer to XP3.5 (below) for more details on establishing pull criteria.

Making the replenishment commitment point explicit brings clarity and transparency in the decision-making process.

Refer to FL2.1 (page 135) for more details about conducting Replenishment Meetings.

Core practices

XP3.5 Establish pull criteria.

The pull criteria define the conditions that have to be fulfilled for a work item to enter the kanban system.

Description

- Identify what needs to be true about a piece of work so as to give it a high probability of flowing without blocking, and an extremely high probability of it not being aborted.

- Achieve consensus on pull criteria with upstream stakeholders.

- Revise pull criteria periodically or as needed.

XP3.6 Establish a delivery commitment point.

Kanban systems have two commitment points: replenishment commitment point and delivery commitment point. Distinguishing the two commitment points allows the team and the management to separate the constraints that they have to take into consideration at each point of the process.

While the focus of the Replenishment Meeting is on understanding customers' and stakeholders' needs and selecting work items to be pulled into the system, the central point of interest at the delivery commitment point is integrating the finished work items into a release and planning and coordinating the deployment process. Delivery commitment will generally be agreed at a Delivery Planning Meeting. Replenishment Meetings make work commitments, whereas Delivery Planning Meetings make delivery date commitments. Different attendees' roles and profiles are needed to conduct these separate decisions. It is also common for the meeting cadences to be different. The transaction and coordination costs of delivery constrain and define the delivery planning cadence, and these costs are unlikely to be the same as the transaction and coordination costs for a selection decision at a Replenishment Meeting. Therefore, decoupling replenishment from delivery planning makes sense and improves agility.

Description

- Identify the point in the process at which incomplete work items are sufficiently complete such that a high-confidence forecast can be made regarding the remaining lead time.

- Some deliveries require preparation and logistics. Ensure that these are identified for any given work item in-progress. Preparation time for accepting delivery may affect the delivery commitment point for specific work items. If a long time is required to prepare a delivery, then an earlier commitment will be necessary. Naturally, this adds risk.

- Decide the following aspects related to managing and improving the team's delivery capability:

  o What criteria have to be fulfilled to ensure that delivery can be made?

  o What post-delivery conditions have to be fulfilled and what risks do these entail?

  o Who has to be involved in the Delivery Planning Meeting?

  o What metrics will give insight into the delivery capability? Lead time, delivery rate, and so on

XP3.7 Establish customer acceptance criteria for each work item or class of work items.

Customer acceptance criteria ensure that customer expectations are properly understood for a given product or service. They remove ambiguity and prevent misunderstandings with respect to customer satisfaction.

Description

- Define customer acceptance criteria for each work item type.

- Customer acceptance criteria have the following characteristics:

  o Define a set of conditions to be fulfilled by the product or service in specified scenarios o Define the scope boundaries of the work item to be processed

  o Determine what kind of tests have to be performed on the work item to ensure it meets customer expectations

- Make sure that the customer acceptance criteria are defined, agreed, and understood equally by the team and the customer.

XP3.8 Define classes of service.

A class of service is defined by a set of policies that describe how a piece of work should be treated. The intent of defining classes of service is to better manage customer satisfaction by tuning the service level to the customer's expectations and business priorities. Offering a variety of classes of service improves risk management and economic outcomes.

Description

- For each class of service, define the policies to be used for selecting and processing work items while they are in the kanban system. These can be related to risks of delay or cost of delay, the organization's image, or other business criteria.

- Four archetypes of classes of service are widely used:

  o Standard – The largest portion of the work should be in this class, typically first-in, first-out (FIFO) queuing or "earliest start date first" selection criterion.

  o Fixed date – There is a hard date beyond which there is a severe cost of delay, such as: a fine, a concrete expense, a lost business opportunity, or another reason for which the cost of delay increases drastically and therefore becomes unacceptable for the organization. Queuing discipline, selection, and pull are judged (usually qualitatively) against the delivery date. Items are effectively given a higher priority if there is a strong chance of missing the required delivery date. There is a tendency to delay starting fixed date items until "just-in-time," deferring commitment until they must be given priority in order to be completed on time. Deeper maturity organizations may develop quantitative means to determine start dates for such work items and choose to start some of them earlier than necessary in order to avoid giving them priority over other items.

  o Expedite – These are very urgent, associated with a high cost of delay. Usually, they are given override or preemptive priority and as many staff and other resources as may be necessary, jumping to the head of every queue, preempting existing work in-progress.

  o Intangible – These are currently low urgency, but important, often involving a severe cost of delay in the distant future. This is work that must be done and is important for long term survival and consistent economic outcomes. Urgency will change in the future if the work is not addressed early.

- For each class of service, establish a threshold expectation for lead time. These have to be based on historical data and customer expectations and must be properly aligned to the business risks they are managing.
  - o A threshold expectation should have two parts: a number of days (or hours) within which the work items should be delivered and a probability or percentage of work items that should hit the expectations, for example, eighty-five percent within thirty days.
  - o It is important that the threshold can be achieved under normal circumstances and only missed due to a specific cause.
- Require that all team members and external stakeholders know and understand the classes of service, their threshold lead times and probabilities, as well as the rest of the associated policies.
- Define how classes of service will be visualized (see VZ3.17 for more details).
- A class of service for an item is selected together with the item when it is pulled into the kanban system.

Maturity Level 4

Transition practices

XP4.1 Explicitly define fitness-for-purpose, and manage based on metrics.

"Fit-for-purpose" implies that a customer's expectations are met by a product or service with respect to a specific purpose they held when placing the order for a piece of work.

Description

The Fit-for-Purpose Framework defines three dimensions for fitness-for-purpose, namely, design, implementation, and service delivery.

For each of these three dimensions, there should be fitness criteria. These are selection criteria that the customer uses to choose one product or service over another.

Each fitness criterion should have a threshold level that represents "fit," and therefore selection of the product or service or satisfaction with the product or service delivered.

For design, each feature, component, sub-system, assembly, or whole, should have a level of nonfunctional quality with a threshold that represents "good enough." Optionally, an additional threshold that represents "beyond expectations" may also be present. Each feature needed for a given purpose defines a function requirement and in turn, each feature should have a quality or fidelity threshold representing an acceptable level of performance.

The nonfunctional, cross-functional, or fidelity definitions represent the required implementation level. Service delivery will have criteria such as lead time, predictability, and timeliness with their own thresholds.

For each market segment, where segments are defined based on customer's purpose, there should be an explicit set of fitness criteria that define the threshold of "fit-for-purpose."

In Kanban, each work item type defines or represents an offered service. Hence, we'd expect explicit fitness criteria for each work item type. Each class of service represents the service level required to mitigate the risks associated with a particular customer's purpose. Hence, we'd expect a set of fitness criteria for each class of service.

Hence, we can create a two-dimensional matrix with work types in each row, classes of service in each column, and a set of fitness criteria in each relevant cell in the table.

Class of service	Standard	Expedite
Work Item Type A	[Fitness criteria for work items of type A, delivered with standard class of service]	[Fitness criteria for work items of type B, delivered with expedite class of service]
Work Item Type B		
Work Item Type C		

Core practices

XP4.2 Establish demand-shaping policies.

Description

A demand-shaping policy is a statement restricting the quantity and arrival rate of a given type of work or class of service. It is generally done to facilitate capacity allocation for work of different types or different classes of service where there is contention—or a deliberate design choice—to create a shared resource or labor pool servicing multiple customers with a variety of demand types and classes.

Examples

- Any given customer shall be limited to three expedite class of service requests per calendar quarter.

- Bug fixes will be limited to thirty per month

Demand shaping policies help create balance. They provide risk management by balancing a portfolio of risk classes in the work-in-progress pool. They focus triage discipline down to a level of individual types of work or specific classes of service. As a consequence, they create stress that drives behavioral change.

For example, a restriction of three expedite requests per quarter may cause an organization to be more proactive and take orders or make requests earlier such that work that historically might have been expedited at the last moment is actually started early and completed using standard service levels. Such restrictions often result in not just limiting expedite requests to three per quarter, rather they reduce them to less than three on average. This is explained through deferred commitment. Customers, product managers, service request managers, and product owners, knowing that their allocation of expedite requests is limited, hold on to them until as late as possible. They will try hard to start other work early, knowing that they hold an expedite request up their sleeve for some late-breaking important and urgent opportunity that arises toward the end of the quarter. If such opportunities never materialize, then the available expedite request goes unused.

XP4.3 Establish SLA on dependent services.

In order to maintain stability of flow in a kanban system that creates dependent work to other services, it is necessary to limit the WIP waiting for any given dependent service. As illustrated by Little's Law, in order to set a WIP limit, we need some consistent expectation of lead time from the dependent service.

Description

Gather historical data from requests sent to the dependent service. Plot a histogram or probability distribution function (PDF) of the lead time data. Lead time should be measured from commitment, usually submission by mutual agreement, until the finished work is delivered back for integration. From this data, a service level expectation may be established or by mutual agreement a service level agreement made.

Maturity Level 5

Core practices

XP5.1 Align strategy and capability.

Description

Strategy—the services offered and the customers or market segments targeted with those services—should be aligned to capability. A failure to align strategy and capability implies that the organization is set up for failure.

Misaligned strategy and capability happens when current capability is insufficient to meet customer expectations. The customer would find the product or service unfit-for-purpose.

Misalignment of strategy and capability can happen in any of the three dimensions defined in the Fit-for-Purpose Framework, namely, design, implementation, and service delivery.

If, for example, our current product doesn't have a design feature our customers expect, then the product is unfit and may not be selected. If it is selected despite being unfit, that may be due to some additional factor such as loyalty, lock-in, network effect with some other integrated product or suite of products, regulation, contractual obligation, and so forth. When a product or service is unfit-for-purpose but the customer continues to select it due to any of these other factors, we can say that the product or service is unhealthy and its life expectancy is (severely) diminished. The product or service and the product unit or business delivering it are fragile.

The same can happen with implementation, our skill or ability to make or offer something with sufficient fidelity to satisfy customer expectations, and with service delivery, our ability to meet expectations for lead time, predictability, and timeliness.

If we fall short in any one of these areas of design, implementation, or service delivery, customers may perceive the product or service as unfit-for-purpose and the vendor as unreliable. This is a fragile, shallow maturity position—risk is high and life expectancy of the product or service will be short.

Customers or market segments should be selected based on our ability to meet expectations for design, implementation, and service delivery. In general, new capabilities—new design features, new implementation capability, or new service delivery capability—should be developed before targeting a segment or a specific customer with expectations beyond our current capability.

When an organization is set up for failure due to an overly ambitious strategy, targeting segments and customers whose expectations we can't yet meet leads to stress. The stress on the organization can prompt heroic effort at the individual or managerial level. These are maturity level 1 and 2 behaviors and hence, indicators of fragility. Alternatively, the organization will be stressed economically through the need to compensate for lack of capability. Compensation—such as reducing prices, slashing margins, or offering sweeteners such as points for a customer loyalty scheme or bundled offers that amount to discounts—effectively eats into margins and affects economic performance. It is hard, perhaps impossible, to achieve maturity level 4 with a misaligned strategy. An optimizing level of economic performance, maturity level 5, cannot be achieved without a properly aligned strategy and capability.

In maturity level 5 organizations, capability leads strategy. Strategies are chosen based on current capabilities or planned capabilities where there is strong confidence that a sufficient level of capability will be achieved.

Methods to strengthen capability include recruiting better skilled people with existing track records of greater capability in performance—for example, when Apple recruited a better designer for the Apple Watch—training, rehearsal and repetition, process improvements, automation, upgrading equipment, and so forth.

Deeper maturity organizations are generally better at identifying gaps in capability and strengthening capability in a targeted fashion to fill the gaps.

9 | Implement Feedback Loops

Goal

Enable comparing expected and actual outcome and use the obtained feedback to evolve further the process and the policies.

Benefits

- Establishes coherent management of the entire process
- Develops unity, alignment, and shared purpose
- Develops short-term shareholder focus
- Develops long-term shareholder focus

Specific Practices Summary

Maturity Level		Implement Feedback Loops (FL) Practice
ML0	Core	FL0.1 Engage in personal reflection.
ML1	Transition	
	Core	FL1.1 Conduct Kanban Meeting.
ML2	Transition	
	Core	FL2.1 Conduct internal team Replenishment Meeting. FL2.2 Hold a Team Retrospective.
ML3	Transition	FL3.1 Conduct Replenishment Meeting. FL3.2 Conduct Suggestion Box Review. FL3.3 Conduct System Capability Review.
	Core	FL3.4 Conduct Delivery Planning Meeting. FL3.5 Conduct Service Delivery Review. FL3.6 Conduct Options Review (upstream).
ML4	Transition	FL4.1 Conduct Risk Review. FL4.2 Conduct Portfolio Review.
	Core	FL4.3 Conduct Operations Review.
ML5	Transition	
	Core	FL5.1 Conduct Strategy Review.

Specific Practices Descriptions

Maturity Level 0

Core practices

FL0.1 Engage in personal reflection.

The intent of the personal reflection is to help an individual learn from her own experience and improve.

Description

- Review the tickets of the finished work items and consider what factors influenced work execution.

- Consider whether the priorities allow for balance between work needs and emotions.

- Consider what caused exceeding established WIP limits and whether it was a justified action.

- Consider whether the size of the tickets is small enough to allow seeing progress with the work and with identifying potential problems soon enough.

- Check if all work was visualized on the board.

- Reflect on other aspects that influence your work.

- Identify improvements and take appropriate actions.

Maturity Level 1

Core practices

FL1.1 Conduct Kanban Meeting.

The intent of the Kanban Meeting is for each person involved in the service or workflow to reflect on the progress of work and the effectiveness of the kanban system.

Description

- Hold the Kanban Meeting daily, at the same time, to coordinate the work within the team and to facilitate self-organization.

- Conduct the meeting in front of the kanban board. Make sure that all team members update the status of their work items and show it on the board before the meeting.

- Walk the board from right (the part that is closest to completed work) to left (the part of not started work).

- Keep the Kanban Meeting short by focusing the conversation on completing work items and resolving issues such as possible delays, technical problems, lack of information, and so on.

- Treat issues that require more time after the meeting, involving only the team members that can contribute to resolving them.

Maturity Level 2

Core practices

FL2.1 Conduct internal team Replenishment Meeting.

The intent of the internal Replenishment Meeting is to select from the backlog work items to commit next, and to replenish the queue for the delivery kanban system.

The typical cadence of this meeting is weekly, or as needed, based on the arrival rate of new information. At an internal team level, the meeting is usually facilitated by the team leader or the person who is in contact with the customer.

Description

- Present information about work items ready to be pulled into the system.

- Discuss dependencies on other work items and technical risks associated with the implementation of the new tickets.

- Identify information needed to facilitate the implementation.

- Make decisions about what to pull next and replenish the Next to start column.

FL2.2 Hold a Team Retrospective.

Team Retrospectives are conducted with regular frequency; the intent is to allow the team to reflect on how they actually manage their work and how they can improve.

Description

There exists a variety of techniques for accomplishing Team Retrospectives. The general guidelines for conducting a retrospective meeting include the following:

- Make retrospectives frequent enough so that the team still has a clear picture of what happened since the previous meeting.

- Limit the meeting to one hour.

- Make it in front of the kanban board, focusing on the completed work items.

- Brainstorm practices and occurrences or facts that fall into some of the following categories:

  o Enjoyable/useful/worth repeating
  o Annoying/not useful/avoid, if possible
  o Missing/consider doing
  o Ideas/worth exploring further
  o Related to current policies (see IE2.2, page 149)
  o Related to sources of dissatisfaction (see IE2.1, page 148)

- Categorize the collected feedback.

- Define improvement actions to be taken.

Maturity Level 3

Transition practices

FL3.1 Conduct Replenishment Meeting.

The Replenishment Meeting is one of the seven Kanban cadences. It happens periodically at the replenishment commitment point (see FL3.1) of the kanban system. Its purpose is to decide together with the customer and/or the stakeholders which work items will be selected and processed for the next period (until the next Replenishment Meeting).

Description

- Prepare the Replenishment Meeting. [1]

- Decide who has to participate: customer, decision-makers, relevant stakeholders.

- Establish what input each participant has to bring to the meeting.

- Establish what options are available and will be discussed at the meeting.

- Establish place and time of the meeting.

- Conduct the meeting at the previously determined place and time.

- Document decisions: document which options were chosen, based on what criteria, and alternative analysis methods.

- Perform studies, or further discussions, related to the evaluated options after the meeting, involving only the people who can contribute to them. The results out of these complementary meetings are made available to the other participants in the Replenishment Meeting.

FL3.2 Conduct Suggestion Box Review.

The concept of an employee suggestion box is an old idea. In a Kanban implementation, it tends to take a more visual form. Perhaps it is a lane on a kanban board for work such as process improvements or improvement suggestions, or perhaps just as a visual bin for collecting the suggestions. There may be a WIP limit or capacity allocation for process improvements in-progress.

A Suggestion Box Review is effectively a triage meeting for selecting which improvement should be implemented now, versus later, or not at all. Hence, it is special version of a Replenishment Meeting. Attendees will tend to be internal to the workflow or service delivery, and it is possible that the entire team may participate.

Description

- Examine new suggestion tickets, each in turn.

- If there is one or more kanban free, then some of the suggestions can be selected to be implemented now, while others will be triaged for later, and left on the board, or for not at all, and discarded.

- Evaluate each suggestion for its impact on the overall performance of the system and the nature of the cost of delay if the improvement isn't implemented. Does the impact rise over time, and if so, is the rise linear or non-linear?[12]

FL3.3 Conduct a System Capability Review.

The intent of the System Capability Review (SCR) review is to examine and improve the effectiveness of a selected service. SCR is a degenerate form of service deliver review (SDR) (FL3.5). The difference is that an SCR is inward facing and looks at capability in isolation, without considering customer needs or expectations. With an SCR, more is usually better, and the intent is to become as effective as possible.

System Capability Reviews compare current capability with defined target conditions. At this level of fidelity and maturity, we are less concerned with where the target came from—it may simply be a goal set by a manager to encourage improvement. Tying objectives to real business risks and customer expectations emerges at the SDR level of fidelity described in FL3.5.

An SCR is typically held twice a month, facilitated by the service delivery manager or his or her immediate superior. Other participants are typically the workers from the service delivery workflow. There is little or no external representation at the meeting.

Description

- Prior to the meeting, review progress and system capability data reported at daily Kanban Meetings and metrics derived from the kanban board or tracking system.

- During the meeting, compare current system capability against a defined target condition; discuss possible actions that allow balancing demand and capability as well as hedging risks appropriately.

- Define actions.

- Prepare feedback for Operations Review and communicate decisions.

Core practices

FL3.4 Conduct Delivery Planning Meeting.

The intent of the Delivery Planning Meeting is to monitor and plan deliveries to customers. It occurs at the second commitment point of a kanban system, at which the team commits to releasing finished work on a specific date.

---

12. A full discussion of cost of delay is deferred to the KMMX for ESP (Kanban Maturity Model Extension for Enterprise Services Planning).

The periodicity of this meeting depends on the planned delivery cadence.

Typically, a service delivery manager (SDM) facilitates the meeting. Any other interested parties should be invited, including those who receive and accept the delivery, and anyone involved in the logistics of making a delivery. Specialists are present for their technical knowledge and risk-assessment capabilities. Managers are present so that decisions can be made as soon as possible.

Description

- Prior to the meeting, review the state of the work items that are potentially available to deliver. Information about this comes from the daily Kanban Meeting. In addition, review feedback from Risk Review meetings to assess how it could affect delivery.

- During the meeting, for the current state of the work items on the board, forecast which of them will be ready for delivery before the release date. Do the forecast based on the established estimation method, for example, Monte Carlo, or using the group's opinion.

- For tickets near the margin of confident delivery, re-evaluate the probability of finishing them by the release date.

- For the in-progress tickets that the team is able to deliver within the schedule, change their class of service to fixed date to include them in the release.

- Taking into account the above-mentioned considerations, make the final decision of which work items will be released. Prepare the feedback for the next risk management meeting.

FL3.5 Conduct Service Delivery Review.

The intent of the Service Delivery Review (SDR) review is to examine and improve the effectiveness of a selected service. It is typically held twice a month, facilitated by the service delivery manager. Other participants include the corresponding service request manager, representatives of delivery teams, customers, and other external stakeholders, if necessary.

Description

- Prior to the meeting, review progress and service performance data reported at daily Kanban Meetings and decisions made at Operations and Risk Reviews.

- During the meeting, compare current service delivery capability to customer expectations and other fitness criteria metrics; analyze shortfalls and causes for not meeting service level expectations; discuss possible actions that allow balancing demand and capability, as well hedging risks appropriately.

- Define actions.

- Prepare feedback for Operations Review and communicate decisions.

FL3.6 Conduct Options Review (upstream).

The intent of the Options Review is to understand the status of the options on the discovery kanban board and select those that have to be moved across the commitment point and those to be elaborated (analyzed or synthesized) further.

Typical participants in the Options Review are the customers or their representatives.

The frequency of the review can be bi-weekly or monthly and has to be established based on the transaction and coordination costs associated with conducting the review.

Description

- Walk the discovery board from right to left.

- Identify the options that are ready to be committed. Take into account the following aspects when making the selection:

  o Proper diversity of options of each work type or customer
  o Available capacity of the delivery kanban system
  o Dependencies between options
  o Important dates and delivery times

- Make sure that enough options are selected to guarantee that the delivery kanban system does not starve. Likewise, select just enough options to avoid discard.

Maturity Level 4

Transition practices

FL4.1 Conduct Risk Review.

The intent of the Risk Review is to understand and respond to risks to effective delivery of product and services.

This review is typically held monthly and facilitated by a service delivery manager, director, or, alternatively, by a Kanban coach. Other participants include anyone with information or experience of recent blockers, project and program managers, customer-facing managers, and managers from dependent services.

The scope of the review is one or more kanban systems, similar to the Operations Review.

Description

- Prior to the meeting, review issues from previous Operations Review, Service Delivery Review, and Delivery Planning Meetings.

- During the meeting, cluster the identified issues, analyze their likelihood and impact, prioritize them based on the expected impact, and discuss risk mitigation or contingency plans.

- Define relevant actions that will improve flow, predictability, and customer satisfaction. These might affect the established kanban systems' design, policies, and classes of service.

- Communicate decisions as appropriate and make sure that affected artifacts (kanban system designs, policies, etc.) are properly updated.

FL4.2 Conduct Portfolio Review.

The objective of the Portfolio Review is to select products and services to be developed and implemented during the next planning period. The selection is made based on the product or service's alignment with the company strategy, dependencies between the products and services, associated risks, and available capacity.

Portfolio Reviews are typically held monthly and the usual participants are portfolio manager, senior management of product and service areas, service delivery manager, functional managers, and product managers.

The portfolio review discussions and decisions are based on input information as follows:

- Status of the products and services in progress

- Business priority information from Strategy Review

- Product and service priority information from product and service delivery managers (based on customer needs)

- Identified dependencies among products and services

- Risks

- Needs for shared resources

- Available capacity reported by functional managers

Description

- Look at dependencies between multiple product developments and services. Evaluate how they affect the development of the expected results (time, cost, quality, customer satisfaction, achieving a strategic goal).

- Evaluate alternatives for resolving the identified problems.

- Identify and evaluate the risks associated to the ongoing and next-to-start products and services.

- Revise product and service prioritization criteria.

- Select products and services that are the best use of the available budget according to the company strategy.

- Assign actions to the managers.

Core practices

FL4.3 Conduct an Operations Review.

An Operations Review is intended to cover a network of interdependent services, a systems-of-systems–level review. Typically, the scope of an Operations Review covers the work of 150 to 450 people, a product unit, a business unit, or a large department or function within an enterprise.

Operations Reviews are a level up from Service Delivery Reviews. The primary focus should be on the interactions between services rather than the independent service nodes within the network. Operations Reviews should be outward looking and business focused. The intent is to ask, who are our customers? what do they ask of us? what are their expectations and why? as well as, how well do we serve them? do we meet their expectations?

Operations Review is, like Service Delivery Review, a disciplined review of demand and capability. At this level, demand and capability are examined for each kanban system within a dependent network of services. There should be a particular focus on dependencies and dependent effects.

Operations Review is only relevant when the scope is large enough and at least more than one kanban system exists.

It is recommended that Operations Reviews happen monthly. A balance must be struck to establish the right cadence. Too often carries too much overhead, and there is little learning from one meeting to the next, while insufficiently often is also problematic. When meetings aren't held often enough, there is too much to discuss and the meeting gets too long, while attendees struggle to have strong memories of events several months earlier. The frequency also affects the effectiveness of the feedback loop. Waiting too long between Operations Reviews means longer before action can be taken to correct an undesirable effect. Empirically, one month has emerged as the best default cadence. There have been examples of every two weeks, six weeks, two months, or quarterly, but monthly is the recommended starting frequency.

Operations Review should be hosted and facilitated by a service delivery director or a vice president responsible for the product or business unit being reviewed.

Participants should include service delivery managers and service request managers for each kanban system; senior management with responsibilities beyond the product or business unit being reviewed; head of PMO; senior business owners or customer representatives; downstream mid-level managers—those accountable for receiving completed work; functional managers responsible for activities within the network of services, and senior individual contributors representing each kanban system; and product, portfolio, and project managers.

Establishing policy around who should be invited and attend an Operations Review is an important step in producing an effective review meeting.

Inputs:

- Summary findings from Service Delivery Reviews for all kanban systems in the network

- Business performance information from Strategy Review, such as financial reports and customer satisfaction surveys

- Ongoing improvement initiatives from Risk Review about system-wide changes

Outputs:

- A list of improvement suggestions/actions/decisions or required changes to strategy, with designated owners, sent to Service Delivery Review and to Strategy Review

- Dependent impact on tail risk for a lead time distribution, sent to Risk Review to inform prioritizing risks for reduction mitigation or contingency planning

Intent: The intent of an Operations Review is to

- Look at performance, capability, and dependencies between multiple kanban systems

- Understand dependencies; expose interdependent effects

- Hold *kaizen* events suggested by attendees

- Assign improvement opportunities to managers as last agenda item

An Operations Review is expensive, and it is important that the best use is made of the time and that the meeting runs to schedule. It should be an orchestrated production with a strictly scheduled and timed agenda. The meeting should be recorded by a scribe. It is common for the scribe to be a process coach, but any specifically designated person who is not the facilitator and host is acceptable.

Maturity Level 5

Core practices

FL5.1 Conduct Strategy Review.

A Strategy Review is a regular meeting of senior leaders to review and assess

- Current markets

- Strategic position

- Go-to-market strategies

- KPIs

- Capabilities

- Alignment of strategy and capability

It should be attended by senior executives and representatives from strategic planning, sales, marketing, portfolio management, risk management, service delivery, and customer care.

It is recommended that Strategy Reviews happen quarterly, as many business, political, and economic environments change quickly. The cadence of the meeting should be a matter for its attendees and tuned to specific circumstances. If quarterly isn't the right cadence, the organization must pick a frequency that is appropriate.

How to pick an appropriate frequency for a review meeting? New information should have arrived since the last meeting. No new information implies there is nothing new to discuss. So how fast is new information, relating to strategy, markets, marketing, and capabilities, available to the team who attend the review? Equally, the period between meetings shouldn't be so long that the quantity of material to discuss, review, analyze, and act upon is so great that the meeting takes too long—days rather than hours. So, a balance must be struck, often enough that the meeting isn't too much of an overhead and burden on attendees, but sufficiently spaced such that new and valuable information is available to discuss. Quarterly is a good default frequency in the absence of analysis on information arrival rate or experiencing the meeting as burdensome. The cadence of a Strategy Review meeting can be adjusted dynamically based on experience and tuned to the business, market, political, and economic conditions within which an organization is operating.

A Strategy Review agenda should include

- Analysis of corporate identity (who are we?)

- Analysis of risk exposure by service, product, or business unit (how resilient is each part of our business?)

  o Fragile

- o Resilient
- o Robust
- o Antifragile

- Survivability assessment

  - o Is our identity still relevant and will it continue to be so?
  - o If our identity needs to change, under what time frame, and how might we go about it?
  - o If we are in the midst of a strategic shift in corporate identity, how is it progressing and is the intended result still relevant?

- Market segmentation analysis

  - o Which markets are we in?
  - o Which segments do we serve, and with which products or services?
  - o In each segment are we a leader/innovator or a follower?
  - o What is our strategic position in each segment? Are we differentiated? A cost leader? A niche player protected by a high barrier to entry? Or are we "stuck-in-the-middle" with a clear position?

- Fit-for-Purpose assessment (see below)

- Capability assessment (from the Operations Review)

  - o Current markets
  - o Strategic position
  - o Go-to-market strategies
  - o KPIs
  - o Capabilities
  - o Alignment of strategy and capability

- Strategy versus capability review

  - o How well aligned is our strategy to our capability?
  - o Are our people set up for success?
  - o Is our strategy within our capability or are we overreaching?

As shown on the list above, a Strategy Review may include a Fit-for-Purpose review. If the Fit-for-Purpose Framework is in use within the organization, it will provide information regarding customer purpose, market segmentation, fitness criteria for customer selection, and thresholds for customer satisfaction. Based on customer surveys or frontline reporting via customer narrative clustering, each market segment can be analyzed to see which are well served, over-served, or under-served. Equally, determine whether target segments are well-served, over-, or under-served, and whether non-targets—customers that we were not expecting—are well-served, over-, or under-served.

The Fit-for-Purpose review enables strategic decisions about market segmentation, targeting, and market actions to encourage or discourage specific segments, such as adjusting pricing, or where to target advertising spending.

10 | Improve Collaboratively, Evolve Experimentally

Goal

Build a shared comprehension of the purpose, process, and associated problems; suggest improvement actions based on scientific models; and reach agreement by consensus in order to evolve continually.

Benefits

- Learn in the process of defining an improvement experiment—predict the outcome—compare actual and expected results.

- Understand the impact of taken decisions.

- Improve risk management at all organizational levels.

- Continually develop the fit-for-purpose capabilities.

Specific Practices Summary

Maturity Level		Improve Collaboratively, Evolve Experimentally (IE) Practice
ML2	Transition	**IE2.1** Identify sources of dissatisfaction. **IE2.2** Identify problematic policies.
	Core	
ML3	Transition	**IE3.1** Suggest improvements using a suggestion box. **IE3.2** Identify sources of delay.
	Core	**IE3.3** Analyze blocker likelihood and impact. **IE3.4** Analyze lead time tail risk. **IE3.5** After meetings: discuss a problem spontaneously, and bring it to the Service Delivery Review.
ML4	Transition	**IE4.1** Develop qualitative understanding of common versus special cause for process performance variation.
	Core	**IE4.2** Identify the impact of shared resources. **IE4.3** Identify bottleneck and resolve it. **IE4.4** Identify transaction and coordination costs. **IE4.5** Develop quantitative understanding of common versus chance cause for process performance variation.
ML5	Transition	
	Core	**IE5.1** After meetings: Discuss – Suggest – Take actions – Seek forgiveness.
ML6	Transition	
	Core	**IE6.1** After meetings: Take congruent actions with confidence.

Specific Practices Descriptions

Maturity Level 2

Transition practices

IE2.1 Identify sources of dissatisfaction.

Understanding sources of dissatisfaction is fundamental for service design, kanban system design, policy definition, and classes of service offered. If this is done properly, the result should be services that are fit-for-purpose.

Description

Identifying sources of dissatisfaction is done in two steps:

- Identify reasons for customer dissatisfaction: why the customers are unhappy, what they complain about.

- Identify internal sources of dissatisfaction: what prevents teams and individuals to deliver professional results and meet customer expectations or what affects their personal job satisfaction.

Once the sources of dissatisfaction have been identified, define appropriate actions for addressing them. Changes to service interfaces such as the Replenishment Meeting may be necessary. Or changes to the kanban system design and the policies that define it may be needed. This may include changes to classes of service or to definitions of pullable, ready, and so forth. On occasion, dissatisfaction may come from poor quality workmanship, and there may be a need for training or new skills and personnel.

IE2.2 Identify problematic policies.

It is common for a service to be governed by a set of policies that have evolved over time. The appropriateness of some of these policies may be questionable, as circumstances may have changed. Often policies are set in isolation, focusing on local improvement without regard to the impact on the whole system.

Visualizing work and managing it transparently brings a better understanding of how outcome is produced and how policies affect decision making and the delivery process.

Team Retrospectives (FL2.2, page 136) and studying the identified sources of dissatisfaction (IE2.1, page 148) allow recognizing policies that might need to be adjusted in order to reduce rework, resolve blocking issues as soon as possible, and speed up delivery.

Maturity Level 3

Transition practices

IE3.1 Suggest improvements using a suggestion box.

The intent of a suggestion box is to democratize insight on system capability and service delivery effectiveness. No one person should have a monopoly on good ideas or insights on system performance. Anyone working in a service delivery workflow or a kanban system should be permitted to submit ideas for improvements.

Description

- Team members have a good enough understanding of the process and are able to identify the need to introduce improvements to it or to the kanban system in order to better satisfy customer expectations.

- Typically, external sources of improvement ideas are sought at this maturity level, such as a coach's advice, trusted literature references, or this model.

- An improvements lane (row) is made on the board. On the left-hand side, an area is set aside as the "suggestion box."

- Anyone can submit a ticket to the suggestion box.

- The ideas are brought to the Suggestion Box Review, FL3.2 (page 137).

- Suggestions selected will then be implemented and their tickets will flow through the lane set aside for improvement suggestions on the kanban board.

IE3.2 Identify sources of delay.

Sources of delay can be classified into the following categories:

- Common (or chance) cause reasons such as queuing, buffering, multitasking, pre-emption by higher class of service work, and so forth

and also

- Special (or assignable) causes such as lack of availability of a shared resource, dependency on another service or external vendor, or waiting for permission, approval, audit, compliance verification, budget approval, and so forth.

Description

Typically, when a piece of work is delayed for a special cause reason, it is marked as blocked, and this is usually visualized with a blocker ticket, decorator, or visual indicator of the blockage (VZ2.3, page 51).

Common cause reasons for delay such as queuing or buffering are not called out or visualized explicitly other than through visualization of the state of the ticket; for example, *Ready for Design* is an indicator that a piece of work is queuing or buffering.

Common cause sources of delay can be identified by analyzing the design or implementation of a workflow. The delay or wait states in the workflow can be identified and potentially flagged or visualized as such. This is a core enabler for gathering flow efficiency data for work items, as flow efficiency requires us to know whether states are wait states or activity states.

Assignable cause sources of delay can be identified by harvesting blocker tickets and analyzing them. It is good practice for blocker tickets to describe the source or reason for delay and record the number of hours or days delayed. Typically, blocker tickets might be harvested from a kanban board once per month and analyzed. The process of analysis has been named "blocker clustering." Sources of delay that are the same or very similar in nature are clustered together with the affinity based in the nature of the delay. This allows for analysis of likelihood and impact of a given source of delay, see IE 3.3, which follows.

A list of known common/chance or special/assignable causes for delay can be maintained with a view to reducing delays by making system design changes, in the case of common causes, and by taking risk management actions, in the case of special causes. The core enabler of improvement in lead time and predictability is a list of known sources of delay. The list should be maintained and monitored regularly, for example, monthly.

Core practices

IE3.3 Analyze blocker likelihood and impact.

Description

- Collect blocker tickets during a period of time, for example, a month.

- Make sure that each ticket records the reason for the blocking and the number of days blocked.

- Classify the tickets by causes, separating internal and external sources of blocking.

- Calculate the average impact of a blocker by cause.

$$\overline{Impact} = \frac{\Sigma_{\substack{all\ tickets \\ per\ cause}} Blocked\ time}{Total\ number\ of\ tickets\ processed\ for\ the\ period}$$

- Calculate the average likelihood.

$$\overline{Likelihood} = \frac{Number\ of\ blocker\ tickets\ per\ cause}{Total\ number\ of\ tickets\ processed\ for\ the\ period}$$

- Use the insights from blocker analysis and the values for $\overline{Impact}$ and $\overline{Likelihood}$ to calculate the magnitude of the risk for a certain event to occur.

$$Risk = \overline{Likelihood} \bullet \overline{Impact}$$

IE3.4 Analyze Lead time tail risk.

The lead time metric indicates how predictably an organization delivers against promises. Understanding the distribution of the lead time for class of service allows evaluating the risk of late delivery.

Description

- Plot the lead time for a work item type or a class of service on a histogram (Figure 42).

  Using a histogram for analyzing the lead time is more useful than using its mean because it provides more complete information about the time it took to deliver work items, including outliers.

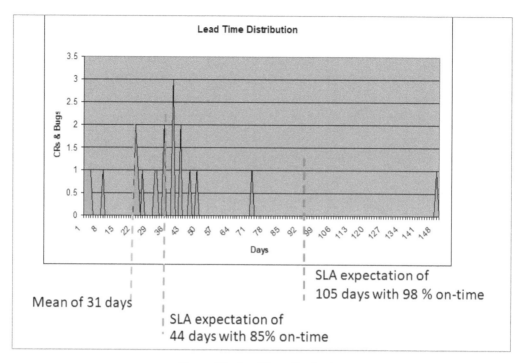

Figure 42   Lead time distribution

- To evaluate the risk of delay, identify what percentage of work items can be delivered within customer expectations. For example, based on the data in Figure 42, eighty-five percent of the work items could be delivered in forty-four days. If this were the customer expectation, evaluate what the risk of delivering fifteen percent of the work behind deadline means to the organization.

IE3.5 After-meetings: Discuss a problem spontaneously, and bring it to the Service Delivery Review.

Description

- After-meetings are conducted by a small group of people involved in the resolution of an issue or an identified weakness in the process or the kanban system design.

- The meetings emerge spontaneously and could occur periodically until a solution or an improvement idea is developed.

- Once defined, the idea is presented to the Service Delivery Review (FL3.4) for further approval and implementation.

Maturity Level 4

Transition practices

IE4.1 Develop qualitative understanding of common versus special cause process performance variation.

Understanding workflow variation and the causes for it is central to improving the performance of the process (system). In general, there exist two sources of variation: internal and external.

Internal sources of variation are those that are under the control of the system in operation: policies, individuals, skills, tools, management decisions. The causes that generate internal variations are known as common causes.

Common/chance-cause variation requires a redesign of the system and can be controlled by means of the kanban board or system design, classes of service, policies, staff training, recruitment, or changes in tool usage

External sources of variation are events that occur and which are out of control of the system. The causes that generate external variation are known as assignable causes.

Special/assignable-cause variation can be controlled by means of risk-management and issue-management strategy and policies. For each special/assignable-cause issue, it should be possible to make a probability and impact assessment and devise risk reduction or risk mitigation to reduce the likelihood, or the impact, or to make contingency plans to undertake in the event of an occurrence. Contingency plans can include temporary fixes, workarounds, or recovery actions.

This is best illustrated by an example . . .

A golf tournament takes place on a course by the ocean on the west coast of Ireland. The course is said to have a par of 72 strokes. This means that on a typical day, a good golfer should complete the 18 holes using only 72 strokes—72 swings of a club, regardless of the design of the club head—wood, iron, putter, and so forth. The designer of the course was most likely a fairly good golfer, and familiar with the weather conditions on the west coast of Ireland. The course design is such that on average, a good golfer should score 72, perhaps over ten to twenty iterations of playing the course.

If we hold a tournament with, say, 100 competitors, and some but not all of them are good golfers, we might expect a range of scores—perhaps from a low of 67 (5 under the par of 72) to a high of 85 (13 over the par score of 72). The average will probably be a couple of shots over par, around 74. This indicates that the course is well designed to offer a suitable challenge to a range of experienced golfers. This spread from 67 to 85 with an average of 74 would be said to be the common cause variation of the course, played by golfers of sufficient standard to hold a handicap ranking and qualify to enter the tournament.

Now, imagine that the tournament is held on a glorious summer day, with hardly a breath of wind, and that this weather was unexpected, following some days of wind and rain. The underfoot conditions are dry, but soft. The golf balls do not run far after impact. In glorious weather, with no wind, and ground conditions that hold the ball reliably, the players can attack the course. Consequently, the best score is a 61 (11 under par, and a new course record), while the average score is 70 (2 under par), and the worst score of the day is 80 (just 8 over par). The skewing of the results is quite obviously a consequence of the beautiful weather conditions, and these conditions can be characterized as special, or assignable, in terms of how they influenced the results.

Equally, on a bad weather day, with howling wind and heavy rain, the scores might be affected in the opposite direction. The best score of the day is 74, the average is 77, and the highest recorded scorecard shows a 95, while some competitors simply failed to return a score at all. Once again, the weather has affected the scores—the range of scores and the average—and once again the weather can be characterized as the special, or assignable, cause or reason for the change in observable behavior.

Description

Developing a skill at qualitative assessment of common versus special cause variation is important.

In the example of the golf tournament on the west coast of Ireland, after the new course record is set on a glorious summer day, should the club pay to have the course redesigned and its level of difficultly increased (usually achieved by making the holes longer and increasing the overall distance for the full course)? The answer, of course, is no. This is intuitive. We understand that the course played easy on an unusually fine day in summer, and it was merely coincidence that the tournament was played on the same day.

We intuitively take the correct action. We do not redesign the system in response to special cause variation.

When the common cause variation is beyond acceptable bounds, then we should re-design the system that produced the observable data. In kanban, this means redesigning the kanban system, changing explicit policies, changing classes of service, WIP limits, work item type definitions, capacity allocations, and so forth. This should only happen in response to obviously common/chance cause variation. When there is a special or assign-able cause variation, we need to take alternative action. We need to use risk assessment and management techniques to determine the likelihood and the impact of an occurrence, and then assess whether we wish to reduce the likelihood, mitigate the impact, or make contingency plans in the event of an occurrence.

All improvement actions, policy changes, and modifications to the design of a kanban system, or a network of kanban systems, including such things as the cadence of a feed-back mechanism such as Operations Review, should be cataloged, and the motivation behind the change documented and classified as common/chance cause or special/assignable cause.

Risk management actions such as risk reduction, mitigation, or contingency should be recorded against the anticipated event, its likelihood, and impact.

There should be clear alignment between risk management interventions addressing special cause variation, and system design changes (policy changes) made to address common cause variation.

Where there has been inappropriate action taken, that is, a system redesign resulted from a special cause variation (W. Edwards Deming classified this as management mistake number two), then a learning opportunity has occurred. Operations Review is a good forum to discuss inappropriate action due to wrongly identifying common versus special cause variation.

When the opposite is true, that there were no changes in the system design and its explicit policies when undesirable behavior was clearly a common failing rather than a specific, special, external event out of the control of management (W. Edwards Deming classified this as management mistake number one), then another learning opportunity has occurred.

An organization should strive to eliminate instances of Deming's mistake numbers one and two and show that action and intervention is congruent with the nature of the problem, even when that nature was qualitatively assessed, such as the weather in the anecdotal golf example.

Core practices

IE4.2 Identify the impact of shared resources.

Shared resources are also known as "non-instant availability" resources. They aren't instantly available because they are currently assigned, or utilized, by another service.

The impact of shared resources, or shared services, is primarily delay. There may be a need to buffer work in front of a shared resource activity in order to maximize the throughput of work completed while the resource is available.

Shared resources are often available on a regular cadence, their availability is subject to time-slicing, with each "owner" receiving a slice of time in a given period, for example, one day per week, or one hour per day.

The impact of shared resources can be measured as the period of the availability and the frequency of availability versus not. So, for example, one hour per day, in an eight-hour working day, is sixteen percent availability. The average delay waiting for availability is half a day, and the distribution of delay is Gaussian.

The arrival rate of work and the nature of the arrival rate must be accommodated. For example, if the arrival rate is two items per hour and its nature is both Gaussian and

Stochastic, then we can infer that, on average, fourteen items will arrive during the period when the shared resource is unavailable.

If this impact isn't accounted for in the design of the kanban system, then the system upstream may suffer stoppage and erratic, uneven flow. The throughput of the system will be restricted to just two or three per day, regardless of the cycle time for the activity.

Buffering in front of the shared resource ensures smooth flow upstream, and the daily throughput is limited by the local cycle time and the maximum number of items that can be processed in the one hour of availability.

Buffering non-instant availability of shared resources can be viewed as a symptomatic fix—address the observed symptoms without attempt to address the root cause—the lack of instant availability.

The root cause fix for non-instant availability is instant availability. Such instant availability can be achieved through automation or by providing contingent, slack resources that are instantly available on demand.

A compromise that approaches instant availability is to seek greater or more frequent availability. For example, one hour per day could be changed to two half-hours per day. This will halve the delay impact and halve the buffer sizing requirements. Three periods of twenty minutes per day would be even better. Often, the frequency is determined by the transaction costs of switching, and this will ultimately limit the possible frequency. By separately addressing the transaction costs of switching (see IE4.5), greater frequency may be enabled without the provision of automation or contingent staffing or resources.

IE4.3 Identify bottleneck and resolve it.

Bottlenecks constrain and limit flow. In general, a bottleneck is a point in a process flow where work items accumulate waiting to be processed.

Description

- Identify the bottleneck in the process. There are two ways to identify a bottleneck:
  - There is always a pile of work items in front of the bottleneck while the resources downstream from the bottleneck are regularly idle.
  - The flow is slowest at the bottleneck; therefore, the local cycle time is largest.
- Identify the bottleneck type:
  - Capacity-constrained resources: the resource is unable to do more work. For example, call reception at a call center depends on the number of workers responding on the phone lines; an industrial assembly process depends on the capacity of the people and tools used to integrate machines.

- o Non-instant availability resources: limited capacity due to limited (but usually predictable) availability. For example, administrative personnel who are only available in the morning.
- Exploit capacity-constrained resources by means of actions such as:
  - o Change the policies so as to control better the work done by the capacity-constrained resource. Classes of service can be used for this purpose.
  - o Bifurcation: Ensure that the bottleneck is working on the most important and specific of its tasks and is making steady progress. Delegate other tasks to other resources.
  - o Limit the interruptions of the resource.
  - o Swarm on resolving problems in the bottleneck.
- Exploit non-instant availability resources by means of actions such as:
  - o Improve availability, for example, if a resource is available four hours per day, using two slots of two hours is better than a single slot of four hours.
- Protect the bottleneck, both capacity-constrained and non-instant availability resources by adding a buffer in front of the bottleneck to ensure that there are always enough work items in it to keep the bottleneck busy.
- Subordinate any other actions in the value stream to enable bottleneck exploitation and protection.
- Elevate the bottleneck—this should always be the latest decision because it requires investment and time to implement:
  - o Add more people and tools/machines
  - o Automate (part of) the process
  - o Training

IE4.4 Identify transaction and coordination costs.

Coordination costs are incurred to organize and communicate meetings, batch transfers, deliveries, and the general handoff and progression of work from commitment to final delivery.

Transaction costs represent the costs of holding or attending a meeting, making a batch transfer of work, a delivery, or a handoff down the workflow from commitment to final delivery.

In general, coordination costs and transaction costs are overheads of doing something necessary. Again, in general, we wish to minimize such overheads. Shorter meetings cost less than long ones. If effectiveness of a meeting can be maintained but its length can be shorter, then we've reduced transaction costs. Easier-to-schedule or coordinate meetings are preferable to those that are difficult and time consuming to schedule and coordinate.

Description

- An effective manner to identify transaction and coordination costs is to ask, if this activity is truly value-adding, would we do more of it? If the answer is no, then consider what actions would contribute to reducing setup, cleanup, and meeting time.

- Identify and make an explicit list of coordination costs associated with meetings, feedback mechanisms, batch transfers, deliveries, and hand-offs.

- Identify and make an explicit list of transaction costs associated with meetings, feedback mechanisms, batch transfers, deliveries and hand-offs.

- Consider elements that contribute to costs such as scheduling or setting an agenda, which are both coordination costs. Can these be reduced or eliminated by having a regularly scheduled meeting with a set cadence and a fixed agenda?

- By monitoring the actual incurred costs and actively seeking to reduce costs through suitable policy changes, system design changes, and risk management decisions, transaction and coordination costs are managed.

- These costs should be monitored as a health indicator metric and action should be taken if they exceed a defined limit. Increasing coordination or transaction costs will have a negative effect on lead times, predictability, timeliness, and economic performance.

> **IE4.5** Develop quantitative understanding of common versus chance cause for process performance variation.

Time or run series data showing a rate (or first derivative, of an absolute count) for general health indicators (e.g., heart rate or pulse), improvement drivers, and fitness criteria metrics is examined and annotated with known assignable or special cause events. The data is examined for stability using its volatility (the second derivative of the time or run series) and its turbulence (the volatility of the volatility of the fourth derivative of the time or run series) See Figure 43 for an example. Stable systems should be devoid of turbulence. Periods of time between spikes of turbulence are known as "volatility regimes." It may be possible to determine bounds of variation within a given volatility regime where all the data points are generated by common or chance cause variation in the system performing under normal circumstances. Data points outlying these bounds should be characterized by annotations indicating assignable or special cause events.

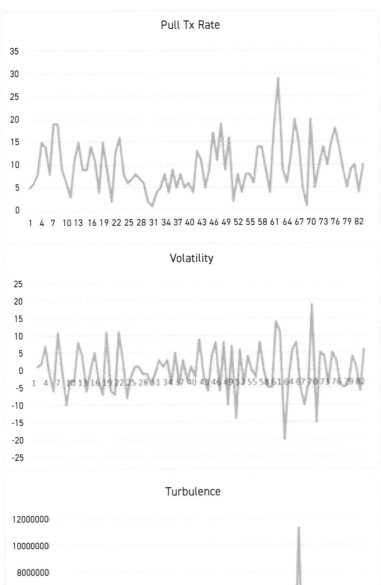

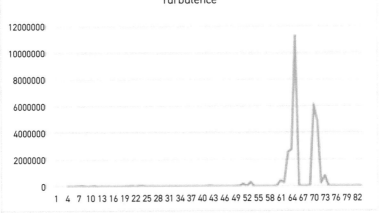

Figure 43   Rate, Volatility and Turbulence diagrams

Attention should be paid to the nature of the recorded data set. There should be a clear understanding of leading versus lagging indicators; for example, WIP is a leading indicator, while lead time is a lagging indicator. With lagging indicators, attention must be paid to the period of the lag and whether an assignable, special cause event happened within that period and had an impact on the value of one or more data points.

The goal should be to define bounds of variation that indicate normal, chance, or common cause variation for the current volatility regime. The result should provide automatic mathematical triggers to indicate out-of-bounds behavior, special cause problems, and/or changes in the volatility regime pre-empted by turbulent data.

Typically, special cause events—outside of the system design and not under its control —or changes to system design will result in turbulence followed by resumption of a new volatility regime. When changes settle in, the system will perform within new limits. A quantitative analysis may reveal the impact of changes that were not recognized or understood. For example, a change to a department manager, without any explicit changes to strategy, values, or policies, may result in turbulence, and, therefore, changes in system performance. When this happens, it is an indication that intangibles are present. For example, the new manager may be seen as soft on discipline and consequently some workers cease to follow policy and operating parameters. Without a quantitative analysis, the very subtle impacts of this loss in discipline may be undetectable.

Maturity Level 5

Core practices

IE5.1 After-meetings: Discuss – Suggest – Take actions – Seek forgiveness.

After meetings refer to the spontaneous assembly of individuals interested in taking action and making changes with a view to improving the performance of the organization. Specifically, the spontaneous assembly is after the Kanban Meeting. In industrial engineering literature, after meetings are often referred to as "spontaneous quality circles" and are seen as self-organizing and self-initiating—there is no specific managerial or leadership role in convening an after meeting. After meetings are not scheduled, nor is there an agenda or invitee list. After meetings are not to be confused with formal approaches to collaborative improvement such as A3 Thinking.

Spontaneous action is taken and reported to more senior managers. Those taking the action seek validation that their action was acceptable, while also reporting that the action has taken place, in order that more senior leaders may know and avoid wasting further time, energy, or resources on the topic.

Description

Following a Kanban Meeting, a group forms with a shared affinity for a recognized problem or process performance issue.

The matter is discussed, evidence (both qualitative and anecdotal as well as quantitative) is presented. Possible options are evaluated. A decision is made, and some of the group accept responsibility to take action, perform a task, or undertake a change.

Once the action is completed, the fact that it has happened, why, and its likely impact is reported to more senior managers.

Maturity Level 6

Core practices

IE6.1 After meetings: Take congruent actions with confidence.

After meetings refer to the spontaneous assembly of individuals interested in taking action and making changes with a view to improving the performance of the organization. Specifically, the spontaneous assembly is after the Kanban Meeting. In industrial engineering literature, after meetings are often referred to as "spontaneous quality circles" and are seen as self-organizing, and self-initiating—there is no specific managerial or leadership role in convening an after meeting. After meetings are not scheduled, nor is there an agenda or invitee list. After meetings are not to be confused with formal approaches to collaborative improvement such as A3.

Spontaneous action can be taken with confidence when strategy, values, and objectives are explicit, institutionalized, and universally understood and supported.

Description

Confident, congruent action can occur when a spontaneously formed group pursues an improvement action in full knowledge that it aligns with strategy, organizational values, and current operating parameters expressed as a set of metrics defining fitness criteria, improvement targets, and health indicators with bounded ranges.

There is no need to seek forgiveness, as it is self-evident that actions are bounded by strategy, values, and current operating parameters.

There is overt trust that those empowered to take action do so within understood constraints, while those taking the action understand that they are empowered to do so, within known and understood constraints.

Individual actions or decisions are never questioned in isolation. When, retrospectively, a failure or poor decision appears to have occurred, the focus is always on redefining strategy, values, or operating parameters, or in better communicating existing strategy, values, and operating parameters.

At maturity level 6, spontaneous congruent action is not validated post hoc by seeking forgiveness, nor is it delayed and validated prior to action by seeking permission. At maturity level 6, action simply happens. If the action taken produces an unsatisfactory outcome, it is succeeded by further action and double-loop learning to examine whether strategy, values, or operating parameters need to change.

In some ways, deep maturity behavior, on the surface, resembles low, shallow maturity behavior—it appears unconstrained. Deep maturity level 6 behavior is characterized by double-loop learning and is always reflecting on outcomes against the framework of strategy, values, and operating procedures and parameters, explicitly defined and broadly communicated.

Part III | Adopting KMM

11 | How to Use the KMM and Why

The KMM is designed to map practice adoption against observable business outcomes, risk management, and leadership behaviors. As such, it offers a codification and a map designed to assist coaches and change agents understand their options. It provides a means to assess, where are we now? how can we consolidate our position? and which path might we follow next? The intent is to provide guidance on practice adoption such that the adoption is successful and in doing so it correctly influences a desirable business, cultural, or economic outcome.

Resistance to Practice Adoption

Why might an organization resist or repel adoption of a specific practice? We have identified a collection of reasons, one or more of which may be present in a given implementation:

- **Identity is being changed or attacked** Adoption of a new practice significantly changes the role and/or responsibilities of one or more people working within the workflow, system, or process; or the presence of the practice is seen as attacking an existing role, and diminishing that role or obviating a skill from which individuals may derive self-esteem, professional pride, or their self-image. For example, if simulation and probabilistic forecasting is introduced, replacing a former planning and estimation practice, the person responsible for leading planning or estimation may feel attacked or diminished by the switch. Alternatively, if such a practice is a tribal ritual associated with the identity of a social group, such as Planning Poker, in Scrum, then an entire team may feel attacked by the suggestion that the need for this ritual is obviated.

- **Fear of incompetence**   An individual may be competent in performing a practice at the current level, but a higher fidelity version of the practice at the next maturity level requires them to learn new skills or gain new knowledge and understanding. The individual fears being seen as incompetent, even temporarily, at this new level and resists adoption. For example, forecasting using linear regression of a mean, assuming Gaussian distribution of data in a sample set, and the applicability of the Central Limit Theorem may be easy to learn and use, and an individual may be competent in its application even if some of the application is inappropriate. Switching to a more robust method of forecasting such as Monte Carlo simulation and using properly sampled reference class data will require the individual to acquire both new knowledge and new skills and a deeper understanding of mathematics. They may resist this for fear of appearing incompetent or for fear of being unable to master the new skill. Loss of mastery affects self-esteem and self-image and results in emotional resistance to adoption.

- **Failure to understand the causation between a practice and an outcome**   For example, achieving maturity level 3 requires that organizations deliver within expectations. This requires that they set expectations appropriately. This will necessitate abandoning existing deterministic, reductionist planning methods that use speculative estimation techniques and replacing them with analysis and probabilistic forecasting methods. A failure to recognize the causation between the failure to meet expectations and the fact that the input to the planning was speculative and without basis in fact reflects core individual immaturity and results in resistance to adoption.

- **Failure to appreciate scale**   Practices that work well on teams of three or four people may hinder larger teams, creating too many lines of communication and too much overhead. Practices that work for a department of thirty may not work for a product unit of 150 or a business unit of four product units numbering 600 individuals. A failure to recognize that the scale has changed, or that practices loved at small scale are not effective at large scale, is again a failure of individual maturity and results in resistance to adoption.

- **Failure to recognize a maturing market and match organizational maturity to the market appropriately**   In an immature, early lifecycle market, technology is emerging, designs are emerging, implementations are emerging, and delivery channels and service levels are all emerging. As a consequence, processes will be evolving and management of them needs to be loosely constrained. In an early market, it is acceptable for product designs to lack the right features, for quality to be poor, and for service delivery to be inconsistent or delivery channels to be unreliable. Early markets may require and reward heroic effort as part of being reactionary to the evolving and emerging nature of the ecosystem in the market. Consequently, the organization may be staffed with individuals who act heroically, are rewarded for it, and heroism becomes core to their identity, their self-image, their self-esteem, and the culture of the organization—they are maturity level 1 people in a maturity level 1 organization, delivering to an immature market. When the market matures, the organization needs to mature with it. Mainstream buyers expect reliability and predictability. They want to work with trustworthy suppliers. If individuals fail to mature and modify their behavior to be congruent with market conditions, then they will continue to behave as maturity level 1 individuals in an organization that now needs to be maturity level 3 or 4. If leaders fail to signal a change in organizational culture and a move away from valuing individual heroics to a more holistic, system thinking, collaborative, aligned organization, then maturity will fail to improve and new mainstream customers will be dissatisfied. Adoption of higher maturity practices obviates the need for heroes, and hence, the heroes resist adoption, feeling it as an attack on their identity.

As a general rule, transition practices do not affect identity or the emotional state of individuals and are safe and easy to adopt. Transition practices for maturity level 3 can be introduced at maturity level 2 in an organization that aspires to maturity level 3. However, the main practices of maturity level 3 are likely to meet with resistance in a maturity level 2 organization.

Transition practices are often designed to lay the groundwork and modify the social conditions to enable the adoption of the main practices for a given maturity level. The main practices are required to deliver the outcome that defines the level, such as "consistency of outcome"—reliable, repeatable, service delivery within customer expectations—that characterize maturity level 3.

Impediments to achieving a next level of organizational maturity are often due to an insufficiency or lack of a sociological or psychological element, or the absence of an important value, in the culture of the organization, such as the following.

- Lack of leadership

- Lack of understanding

- Lack of systems thinking

- Lack of agreement

- Lack of trust or insufficient empathy

- Lack of respect

- Lack of customer focus or service-orientation

- Failure to value flow

Transition practices and the Kanban values are there to mitigate these sociological, psychological, and cultural challenges that impede achieving a subsequent level of organizational maturity. The Kanban values are mapped against the maturity levels on the model and leaders must be prepared to introduce these values to the culture of the organization to enable the next level of depth in maturity.

Breadth of Kanban adoption also helps remove impediments to greater depth of organizational maturity. For example, making policies explicit raises the level of social capital by defining the boundaries and constraints on action. Empowerment is enabled by explicit policies and hence, trust is increased. Thus, as we expand the breadth of Kanban general practice adoption, we anticipate that the depth of organizational maturity will deepen.

Visualization and metrics help with understanding. If the impediment to adoption of main practices at the next level is due to a lack of understanding, then implementing additional visualization or reporting additional metrics that "shine a light" on the problem will help with understanding and create demand for the main practice otherwise resisted. So, additional visualization or reporting practices act as transition practices to implement the main practice.

Visualization and transparency also create empathy and trust. Both empathy and trust are core enablers of everything else.

There may be a need to justify why a group of individuals needs to act as a team. A team may simply be a social group with some affinity around shared identity and some need for accountability or supervision. In this case, we see the aggregated personal kanban pattern.

In other cases, the need for collaborative teamwork comes from a task being too big or too intimidating for an individual to undertake it alone. As soon as we have a need for collaboration, we see the team kanban pattern emerge.

When there is a lack of social capital or social cohesion, transition practices are required to engineer more social capital and the social structure and mechanism to encourage collaboration. We see this with the transition pattern from aggregated personal kanban to a service-oriented, collaborative team kanban, with the renaming of lanes away from individuals to the services provided and work item types processed, together with the use of avatars for multi-skilled, or generalist workers. By implication, a worker with an avatar is seen as socially superior to those who merely have their name on a single row of the board. This creates social pressure to improve and broaden skills within individuals and results in a broader, more skilled, more liquid labor pool. The benefit is faster, smoother flow. What enables this pattern is service-oriented thinking, coupled to the oblique approach of introducing a practice known to socially engineer demand for a desirable outcome—a more broadly skilled workforce, a managerial focus on work to be done, and customer satisfaction, and a move away from managing individuals.

Making policies explicit and defining boundaries and constraints also helps with understanding. A clearer definition of the rules may enable main practices at the next level.

A lack of leadership and a failure to create *Einheit*, unity and alignment behind a sense of purpose, will be an impediment to achieving maturity level 3 or deeper.

A lack of systems thinking will be an impediment to achieving maturity level 2 and this will become more and more acute the deeper the attempted implementation. To achieve levels 3 and deeper, the organization needs to think in terms of systems and systems of systems. Systems thinking and the concept of a workflow as a system to deliver a product or service is a necessary enabler of flow.

A lack of customer focus will be an impediment to achieving maturity level 3. Again, this will become more and more acute the deeper the attempted implementation or the greater the scale of the implementation. To achieve levels 3 and deeper, an organization needs to think in terms of services and see the organization as a network of interdependent services.

A failure to value flow will impede achievement of maturity level 3. Unevenness of flow results in a lack of predictability and an inability to deliver on expectations and promises. This impacts trust, and a lack of trust retards some other practices such as pull and deferred commitment, which are needed to respect WIP limits and maintain a system without overburdening it. A failure to value flow can result in a vicious cycle that causes maturity to regress.

Agreement requires trust, respect, and explicit policies. Without agreement, there cannot be disciplined implementation of WIP limits, which affects flow, resulting in unevenness and overburdening.

Without respect, the operation of the systems and processes is dysfunctional and unreliable. Maturity level 3 cannot be achieved without a cultural value of respect. Some specific practices are engineered to mitigate a lack of respect, or to increase the level of respect, enabling an organization to get to the next level.

In low maturity environments, a lack of respect can be mitigated or countermanded with legislation—explicit policies, strictly enforced. While such countermeasures may be effective in some situations, they don't reflect the core Kanban values.

To achieve maturity level 4, there needs to be respect for the shareholders and the concept that there is a business, an economic entity, which requires making profits in order to exist. Without respect for the owners who have placed capital at risk, there will be scant regard for margins, profitability, cost controls, and so forth. There will be no drive to achieve deep maturity at levels 5 and 6 if the long-term survival of the business isn't explicitly valued. It is common for founders or founding families to value long-term survival. Their interests are aligned with the lowest paid and least mobile of the workforce. It is often the middle managers who are least vested in long-term survival—there is nothing in it for them, no shared interests, and their skill set and relative wealth make them highly mobile and resilient to partial or total business failure. To enable levels 5 and 6, it is necessary that senior leaders align the interests of middle management and give them "skin in the game" of long-term survival. Traditionally, this was done using corporate pension schemes rather than the more common employer-subsidized individual contributor systems preferred in modern businesses. Other approaches typically involve employee ownership, including stock grants or stock options with vesting periods typically exceeding five years. Such systems have had limited success in creating a middle-ranking workforce truly vested in long-term corporate survival. Leaders need to think deeply about how to align the interests of highly mobile, economically secure middle managers if deep maturity is to be achieved and sustained.

Between maturity levels 3 and 4, there is a distinct shift from qualitative measures and decision frameworks to quantitative measures and analysis. In neuropsychological terms, there is a shift to System 2 (logical inference thinking in the pre-frontal cortex) from System 1 (emotional pattern matching in the limbic brain or amygdala). A level of individual maturity is required to enable this transition. In some cases, it will be individuals who impede achieving a deeper level of maturity and from time to time it may be necessary to move or remove individuals who lack the emotional agility to operate comfortably at deeper maturity levels.

References

1. Alexei Zheglov, "Observing Replenishment," www.connected-knowledge.com
2. David J. Anderson, *Kanban: Successful Evolutionary Change for Your Technology Business*, Blue Hole Press (2010)
3. David J. Anderson, Andy Carmichael, *Essential Kanban Condensed*, Lean Kanban University Press (2016)
4. Donald Reinertsen, *The Principles of Product Development Flow*, Celeritas Publishing (2009)
5. Donella H. Meadows, Diana Wright, *Thinking in Systems: A Primer*, Taylor & Francis (2009)
6. Gerald M. Weinberg, *Quality Software Management, Volume 1: Systems Thinking*, Dorset House (1997)
7. Depth of Kanban Assessment Framework, David J. Anderson, London Lean Kanban Days (2013) https://www.youtube.com/watch?v=JgMOhitbD7M
8. Lean Kanban University Glossary, http://edu.leankanban.com/kanban-glossary-terms
9. Mary Poppendieck, Tom Poppendieck, *Lean Software Development: An Agile Toolkit*, Addison-Wesley Professional (2003)
10. Mike Burrows, *Kanban from the Inside*, Blue Hole Press (2014)
11. Mike Burrows, Introducing Kanban Through Its Values, https://blog.agendashift.com/2013/01/03/introducing-kanban-through-its-values/

12. Nassim Nicholas Taleb, *Antifragile: Things That Gain from Disorder*, Random House (2012)

13. Patrick Steyaert, *Essential Upstream Kanban*, Lean Kanban University Press (2017)

14. *CMMI for Development: Guidelines for Process Integration and Product Improvement* (3rd ed.) SEI Series in Software Engineering, CMMI Institute (2011)

15. *A Guide to Project Management Body of Knowledge*, (5th ed.), Project Management Institute (2013)

Index of KMM Practices

Limit Work-in-Progress

Manage Flow

Improve Collaboratively, Evolve Experimentally

Index

About the Authors

David J Anderson is an innovator in management thinking for 21st Century businesses. He is chairman of Lean Kanban Inc., a training, consulting, events, and publishing business, making new ideas accessible to managers across the globe. He has more than 30 years' experience in the high-technology industry, starting with games in the early 1980s. He worked at IBM, Sprint, Motorola, and Microsoft, as well as a number of startup businesses. He is the pioneer  of both the Kanban Method and Enterprise Services Planning.

Teodora Bozheva has more than twenty-five years of experience in the field of software development. She has personally undergone all the challenges in managing large projects and meeting tough schedules with limited resources. For more than fifteen years she has been providing training and coaching based on Kanban, Lean, CMMI and Agile to companies in different industries. With insights and practical guidance she helps them combine and adjust the methods to their unique contexts, improve their management practices, deliver better products and services faster, and adopt continuous improvement culture. Teodora runs Berriprocess, a training and coaching company based in Bilbao, Spain.

Visit **kanbanmaturitymodel.com** and download your free KMM posters (in PDF).

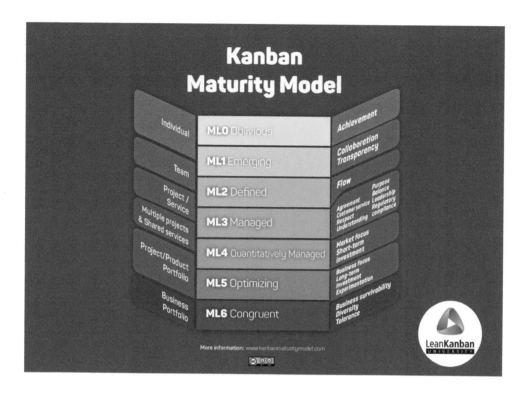

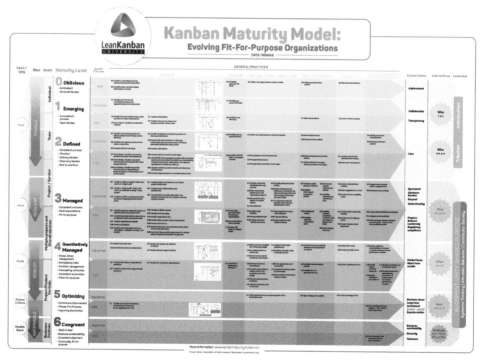

CPSIA information can be obtained
at www.ICGtesting.com
Printed in the USA
FSHW021900081218
54254FS

9 780985 305154